P9-EDU-216

LESSONS

FROM THE

ROAD

MUSICIANS AS
BUSINESS LEADERS

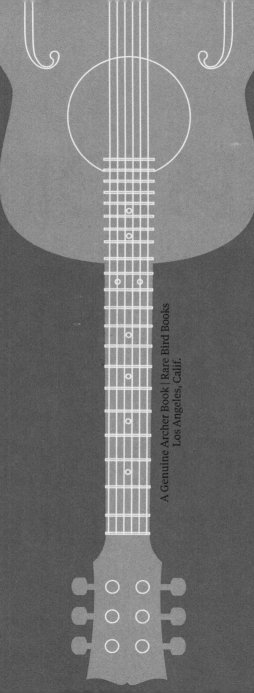

A Genuine Archer Book | Rare Bird Books
Los Angeles, Calif.

LESSONS

FROM THE

ROAD

MUSICIANS AS BUSINESS LEADERS

TODD PASTERNACK

A GENUINE ARCHER BOOK

All rights reserved. No part of this publication may be reproduced, distributed, or transmitted in any form or by any means, including photocopying, recording, or other electronic or mechanical methods, without the prior written permission of the publisher, except in the case of brief quotations embodied in critical reviews and certain other noncommercial uses permitted by copyright law. For permission requests, write to the publisher at the address below:

ARCHER/RARE BIRD

453 South Spring Street · Suite 302 · Los Angeles · CA 90013
rarebirdbooks.com

Copyright © 2017 by Todd Pasternack

FIRST TRADE PAPERBACK ORIGINAL EDITION

Set in Minion
Printed in the United States

10 9 8 7 6 5 4 3 2 1

Publisher's Cataloging-in-Publication data
Names: Pasternack, Todd, author.
Title: Lessons from the road: musicians as business leaders / Todd Pasternack.
Description: First Trade Paperback Original Edition | A Genuine Archer Book
| New York, NY; Los Angeles, CA: Rare Bird Books, 2017.
Identifiers: ISBN 9781941729243
Subjects: LCSH Music trade. | Music trade—Vocational guidance. | Music—
Economic aspects. | BISAC
Classification: LCC ML3790 .P365 2017 | DDC 780/.23—dc23

Musicians tell stories through their songs. Brands tell stories through their products and marketing creative

CONTENTS

*It's tough
to measure
success for
something
that doesn't
exist yet*

PLEASE ALLOW ME TO INTRODUCE MYSELF

DO YOU REALIZE HOW quickly things have changed in the last ten years for marketers? How quickly the pace of innovation has accelerated and ultimately altered the way we think, work, and connect with each other?

Your phone shakes as you pass by a Starbucks to remind you to use your app with a balance of $2.11 on it. A web camera at your local big-box retailer scans your face, stores your faceprint in a database, and knows the next time you walk into their store.

You get an email about the upcoming season of women's clothes from Banana Republic. You click and go the site on your laptop. You quickly check Facebook on your iPhone only to see a Banana Republic ad in your News Feed for the blouse you just zoomed by seconds ago—from your laptop.

You slap on a virtual reality headset and are immersed in another world through surround sound. I mean—you are *there*. You look around this virtual world and walk past a digital billboard with a personalized Coke ad with your name on it.

It's hard to believe that about ten years ago this was all imagination. Fiction.

Now it's part of our everyday. And marketers are carefully trying to stay balanced on a shaking tightrope above the abyss of emerging technologies. Their desire to connect more intimately and personally with consumers is just a tweet or post away from crossing into the creepy zone.

As someone who has been responsible for driving innovation and consulting on emerging technologies, I've been lucky to help shape and contribute to the rapidly evolving digital marketing and advertising industries over these last ten years. I've consulted with some incredible brands like Apple, Microsoft, Ford, Chrysler, Nissan, Target, General Mills, partnered with groundbreaking agencies like R/GA, TBWA\Chiat\Day, CP+B, and worked with cutting-edge technology companies like Facebook, Adobe, and Twitter.

I helped advertisers bring the first interactive ad creative to the iPhone and iPad the day the devices were released to the public. I've worked with advertisers to use their disparate sources of audience data to power personalized creative and messages on every piece of glass someone can stare at, and then measure success in terms of engagement, conversion, and sales. I've shown them how beacons, virtual reality, facial recognition, and even web standards like HTML5 fit into their businesses before they think they need them or ever hear of them in the first place.

But it's no secret that innovation is challenging within any organization. It's not always easy to figure out which technologies are here to stay and which will quickly vanish. It's difficult putting the right people together into teams to create and execute new ideas, let alone instill a belief in those ideas. It's tough to measure success for something that doesn't exist yet.

I often find myself pulling from my own experiences as a former touring and recording musician to help me address these challenges.

Wait, what?

Creating

Experimenting

Recording

PLEASE ALLOW ME TO INTRODUCE MYSELF... AGAIN

LIFE WAS VERY DIFFERENT for me from 1994–2004 than it is today. I'm sure it was for you, too.

Here was my work routine: Get in the van, drive to the venue in the next city, play the guitar and sing my ass off for a bunch of people, pack up the van, drive to the next city. Wash, rinse, repeat. Every night for weeks in a row. For years. This was my *job*.

Some nights I played in front of more than two thousand people. Some nights barely twenty. Big rooms, little rooms. Great performances. Shitty performances. We were signed, but I wasn't famous or anything. You've never heard of the bands I've played in. *Really.*

Feel free to Google me, though.

Once people find out I used to be a full-time touring and recording musician for over ten years,

I get asked the same question: "How the hell did you end up in digital advertising?"

First I say blankly, "The internet." Then after we have a laugh, I explain: I wanted to market myself better than the record label, but I had no idea how to do it. So I figured that if I could record entire albums on my laptop, how hard could it be to learn how to build websites or code a banner ad?

Oh my.

I quickly bought those three-inch-thick coding books to get schooled. Then here's what I didn't expect to happen: I was twelve years old with my first guitar all over again.

It didn't hurt that my dad had been a Creative at a few big agencies in New York—Y&R, Wunderman, and Grey—before ultimately becoming a Creative Group Head at the in-house agency for MBNA (now Bank of America). I was familiar with this world, I just never imagined being a part of it.

I grew up with a closer connection to the brands my dad worked on: Johnson & Johnson, Timex, Canada Dry, JELL-O, Lipton Soup, Frito-

Lay, and Kenner (big score for any kid). He'd let me miss school to join him in the office, go to shoots, and go to the jingle houses.

I'd watch ideas materialize throughout the day with pencils, markers, and thick storyboard paper (this was the seventies and eighties). Those storyboards ultimately fueled pitches to win new business.

When my dad wasn't doing ad stuff, he was home playing the piano or the drums. Creating. Experimenting. Recording.

Build and foster creativity

THE COMMON
DENOMINATOR

As I met and befriended customers on the client side, agency side, and technology-partner side of my business, I picked up on a common love of ours. The people I felt did some of the most inspired work, and truly helped advance their businesses, had this common denominator to them all: music. They were former professional musicians, or still part-time professional musicians, and applied what they learned as musicians to their work as marketers, technologists, and business people.

This was something I hadn't anticipated when I took my hiatus from the music industry.

The "musician-to-marketer" or "musician-to-technologist" thing was—*a thing*.

It got me thinking that there are tangible, valuable business lessons to learn by connecting the ways bands and musicians work, collaborate, fight, and make up together—all to create music—with the way any organization operates to ultimately sell stuff people want and need.

Musicians tell stories through their songs. Brands tell stories through their products and marketing creative.

To create something meaningful and memorable, both bands and businesses need to do similar things:

- Build and foster creativity and innovation

- Collaborate with many personalities and opinions to produce something incredible that connects with people

- Get the best out of teams

- Listen to help make better decisions

- Recognize which opportunities to capitalize on or accentuate

- Determine quickly when it's time to kill an idea

I've noticed that while many musicians may not be thinking in these exact operational concepts or using them every day, businesses often do, and they thrive on them. I've also found the complete opposite to be true: businesses struggling to find success out in market and within their own walls because these core tenets aren't clearly defined or even present.

This is a business book with lessons from musicians.

THIS IS NOT A WORKBOOK.
THIS IS A RECORDING.

OVER THE LAST TWO years I interviewed ten people. Most are from the "business world" and have former, or still very active, lives as professional musicians. They shared how they weave their musical experiences into their marketing/technology/business jobs every day. A couple folks are 100 percent full-time musicians who help show how the music world—completely on its own—is not much different than the "business world" at all.

These diverse, successful people told me their stories as both musicians and business people, dropping nuggets of valuable insights and observations they've made through their own comingling of these two worlds.

Here's the line-up and a few of their recent roles as of this publishing date:

Rob Avery—VP, professional services at Scala/VP, mobile strategy at Digitas Health/guitarist and bass for BoySetsFire and Son and Heir

Jimmy Chamberlin—CEO at Blue J Strategies/CEO at LiveOne/drummer for The Smashing Pumpkins and record producer

Reid Genauer—CMO at Magisto/guitar and vocals for Assembly of Dust

Anurag Gulati—global business development partnerships manager at Uber/global partnerships at Facebook/studio owner and engineer

Cat Kolodij—marketing strategy and experience at Progressive Insurance/SVP, brand planning director at Arnold Worldwide/guitar and vocals for Working

Michael Lowenstern—VP, digital advertising at R/GA/ Group Creative Director at Amazon/bass clarinet

Naomi Margolin—national sales director at Armada Global/vocalist with Sam Moore and Mark Newman Band

Glenn Rosenstein—senior partner & co-owner at Wealthpoint Financial Group/record label president and record producer

Derek Richmond—executive producer of Integrated Production at Prettybird/guitarist

Al Schnier—guitar and vocals for moe

There are valuable business lessons in what these professionals have to say, and I'm sure you'll uncover more by digging deeper. You can collect an arsenal of great musical analogies and stories to take back to your organization and help bring these lessons to life in your own way, within your own company culture. Their "lessons from the road" will help uncover techniques to better examine your business. I bet you'll also find a few things to apply to your personal life. I know I did as I spoke with them all.

Don't worry, you don't have to be a musician to appreciate their stories. Similarly, the teams and people the interviewees work with in a business setting aren't all musicians, but they have all managed to incorporate their experiences from being on the road into these environments. But ask around. You may be surprised how many people in your company are former or part-time professional musicians. I bet the language of music intersects with the language of business within your company more often than you realize.

This book is organized so you can quickly jump to different topics and pick up from anywhere immediately. Just place the needle down anywhere you like. And like any great song, there are many spaces for you to fill with personal meaning and interpretation.

Here's my recommendation: Read this book as if you're listening to an album with headphones on. You're bound to "hear" something new each time.

Enjoy, and rock on.

How do you get everyone to **drink the Kool-Aid?**

START ME UP

Starting bands and businesses: Creating vision, mission, and culture

I STARTED MY FIRST band when I was twelve. A friend of mine came home from summer camp having learned how to play the drums. He said, "You should play guitar" and I answered, "Okay. Guess we should start a band." So we did.

And just like that, I was in that band for almost ten years and that moment literally changed my life.

Bands sometimes start like that. You know, you find a few people who are just as passionate about music and expression as you are. Maybe they're your friends. Maybe not. Maybe you're outcasts. You find a guitarist, a singer, a bass player, and you finally score a drummer. You get together. You jam. And after a few minutes you look at each other, recognizing that something magical just transpired. It may not have been perfect or even good music, but the energy and talent this small group just released in that single moment is bigger than all of you. You agree to play as much as possible, write music nonstop, try to record an album right away, and just make it all happen. No matter what.

There's no looking back.

Now instead of musicians with instruments, what if you had a developer, a designer, and someone who can sell anything? You riff on a big idea that everyone believes can completely change the way people behave. You're almost in disbelief no one else is doing it and you recognize there is a huge opportunity to monetize on it. After a few late-night conversations, plenty of caffeine, shitty food, and a white-board session, you look at each other, realizing you're all in it together and committed to seeing the idea come to life and become a business. There is an undeniable energy that unites everyone.

There's no looking back.

This may describe a story you're familiar with. A few details are probably off, but most likely not by much. There has been an evolution over the last twenty-five years or so around the ways and methods by which people can create together, to make something that moves and inspires others, and to ultimately—potentially—build a business from that passion.

"We celebrate entrepreneurs. And I guess we celebrate super successful corporate executives as well," Reid Genauer says, comparing the origins of bands and businesses. "But we celebrate entrepreneurs as sort of beacons of the American dream. And yet so many of them live out of the context of how nine out of ten people exist.

It's that nonconformist culture that attracts these creative minds.

"And I think that's the direct lineage back to music.

"Because in 1970 when you were sitting in your basement and you were one of these geeky, creative types—antiauthoritarian geeky, creative types—the brightest star shining in front of you was probably rock and roll. It was like, that was what you did. You learned to play the guitar, you joined a band. And what's happened more recently, but it's been a steady evolution, is that a lot of the new rock stars are entrepreneurs. And the same kids who would have been learning to play the guitar—or maybe do, as well—are geeking out in their basement to video games and learning how to build them.

"You can draw parallels between just band dynamics in general and business, and I think there's some strong general pattern recordation. And then there are some I think fit more specifically with start-up culture.

"General pattern recognition is that having a successful band is like having a successful department in any company. Whether it's a start-up or Coke. It takes people with disparate backgrounds, with disparate skill sets, with varying senses of vision and ego to come together and work productively. And it's the hardest thing to do."

The first moments when you get together to jam with musicians that you don't know can be a little uncomfortable. Not "bad uncomfortable," just tough to create a focus to begin somewhere together musically. Are you going to play some Zeppelin? Maybe some My Morning Jacket or

The National? An old bluegrass standard? It takes someone to start playing, to start "speaking" and express an idea of where a song or a jam can go. The rest of the musicians start to contribute musical ideas based on the musical direction articulated by the first person. And while the sounds and notes may change and take different shape over time, it's not uncommon to echo or come back to that first motif as an anchor for the musicians. You can *hear* it when it happens. But you can also *see* it on the musicians faces when they come back to the theme they started from together.

Imagine if everyone jamming just started playing whatever they wanted at the same time. Different keys, different time signatures and styles of music. Most likely, it would be a hot mess of noise. (Unless, of course, the musicians' intent behind their jamming was to do just that, and there was understanding and commitment to that approach from the start.)

In business, it's no different. When there is a strong vision statement or mission, it's easier to play with ideas because they are rooted in something unwavering and concrete. You can go way far out thinking about product and marketing ideas when you have something foundational to build on top of.

Look at Facebook for example. For the last decade, Facebook has focused on making the world more open and connected. Everything centers around this: culture, product development, marketing, and messaging.

Everything.

And while helping people connect and share will always be a huge part of who it is, Facebook also realized that it needed to do more. It also has to work to bring the world closer together. So, the mission expanded to set its course for the next ten years, with a new challenge for itself: give people the power to build community and bring the world closer together.

This is an evolution and response to what Facebook's community now needs from the company, and builds off the original mission. I'd posit here that without the first core mission statement being central to who the company was and became, it wouldn't have been as recognizable of where the company needs to go next.

However, a mission is not easy to create even though it's so critically important to a business, let alone articulate it simply as it embodies everything a company will orbit around. Often times the mission just…happens.Organically. The key is to capture and articulate it as soon as you recognize it's there, because everything and everyone will try to align to it and make it their North Star.

And then once the mission or vision is expressed, how do you get everyone to drink the Kool-Aid? Whether your company is five people, five hundred, or five thousand.

It's hard, right?

Is it because you're trying to instill a belief within people who may not believe you?

And if you do succeed in getting the people around you to believe in your vision and your mission, how do you develop the faith in each other that no one is going to slack, everyone is a contributor, and there is only one direction and one way to move: forward and together.

This agreement—spoken or unspoken— along with how everyone treats each other, sets the tone for a culture right from the beginning.

Alignment of vision and goals influenced the formation and success of The Smashing Pumpkins.

Jimmy Chamberlin reflects on the seriousness of committing to the band: "It really is [serious].

And it's a lot like business, right? [Billy] Corgan and I had long, long, deep conversations about not only the music, but what were our influences, where did we want to take things musically, and what was the general strategy.

"Our thing was like: look, it's fun to be in a local rock band that's doing great and get all of these local accolades. But what Billy and I were really interested in was participating at the highest level. And that was really exciting for me. I thought with him as a songwriter and me as a drummer, it created an opportunity for us to really go live at that highest level. And the music we started creating when I joined the band started to really lend itself to where I was at as a drummer.

"When I joined the band it was very much kind of an R.E.M., kinda jangly pop band. And although the songs were incredibly good, I think if it would have stayed that direction I probably would have left the band. But once Billy heard the way that I play drums, he started to reinterpret his own songwriting and started to build around the drums as a focal point. And that's where songs like 'I Am One' and 'Bury Me,' the songs that on *Gish*, were kind of born of that philosophy.

"That created a really attractive environment for me to both flower as a musician and really make a go of music as a business and an economic solution."

It's not easy to keep on vision.

As marketplaces evolve, your products may start to feel stale and less significant in bringing value. How many times have you considered a pivot? How many times have you weighed that pivot against your core vision and mission to see if it still supported it? Bands share similar pivotal moments in their careers.

Cat Kolodij digs into this a bit: "So often times that first album is a true expression of the vision that you have for your band, and what you're trying to accomplish, and why you've come together to begin with.

"But then you go on the road and you start playing the songs over and over again, and you yourself get bored before other people get bored because [you're] playing the same songs. And sometimes they lose their magic out of boredom. Or out of forgetting why you started in the first place.

"You start to explore and go off on your own. It's what I call 'going off brief,' right? You forget why you're a band in the first place. You're just trying to replicate the success, not the feeling you had when you were writing the songs."

You sometimes lose your way.

Cat's comparison of a vision for a band to a creative brief is spot-on.

Again, articulating a strong vision and mission is hard. Reid talks about his own experience addressing this: "For me, as a musician and as an exec at a start-up, the thing that I brought to the band was the fact that I could sing—so being a voice—and then being able to bring a vision for a song. And we talked about songwriting. Even if that song wasn't completely finished, it was a codified vision.

"And I think that where so many bands struggle, particularly around original music, is [when] everybody can play their instrument but there isn't a vision for the song itself or for the body of work that you're aiming to create. So in my musical life, I've been able to bring that creative vision and to give it a voice quite literally in terms of singing and lyrics.

And in my professional life, it's a similar skill set, which is to be able to offer a vision to a group of people that, from a sea of possibility and confusion, is tangible. And that you can articulate, and that you can be a voice for, and be passionate about. And those are core to who I am and they're kind of soft skills.

"But compared to being able to shred on your guitar, or being able to code, I can't do either of those two things, which are much more tangible and arguably much harder things to learn—well, I don't know if they're harder to learn or not, but they're much more concrete things to learn—and yet, I've been able to incorporate both of those things into my work, both as a musician and as a entrepreneur. But [I've] been able to complement them with some softer skill sets that are also needed."

If you sense the culture isn't strong in your company: address it now. Don't wait another day.

Rob Avery says that when his band BoySetsFire began to abandon its culture and vision as they got more successful—it ultimately triggered him to leave: "If you're not on the same page with the project or an overall company culture, it's going to be disastrous. I've seen it happen. I've seen [situations] where, because folks don't understand the end goal or they don't why they're doing things, that ripple effect can make people leave companies. The passion kind of withers out of them.

"I know that not everyone is passionate about their job, but I think when you have real transparent communication, and the goal and messaging is clear, and your call to arms for what you're doing vocationally is clear, you can build. Inspire. A lack of transparency and communication will do the exact opposite: it will kill momentum, stifle innovation, and be really detrimental."

Rob continues: "So when you're hiring folks you do want to talk about the culture. You do want to talk about the vision. You do want to talk about the momentum and the end goal. If you see the spark in folks' eyes, they're nodding, they're getting it—outside of the technical chops, that's a huge thing in acquiring great talent.

"That translates to the people I'm making music with now. They might not be the most technically proficient—and I'm not saying I am—but they have goals, the same intention. Even though we need to narrow that down and focus it, overall we want the same thing out of this."

Al Schnier says his band moe. figured this out pretty early on: "One of the things that is not unspoken is that we've always maintained that if we do work for moe. in any capacity—whether you're in the band, in the crew, whatever—that you're representing moe., and that more or less we want to be regarded as band that is easy to work with and agreeable and willing to cooperate in various situations."

Company culture should eventually emanate from every direction, but it starts from the top. It must be defined and maintained from the beginning and embodied by each founding member. It builds unity and creates an easier way to operate within the band or business as it grows. And like Al says, it starts with the hiring process. Rob agrees:

"I have tried to capture it.

It's not about the free lunches, or the ping-pong table, or the fact that we got iPads as a holiday gift.

"That to me is not culture. But it seems to be what folks focus on, especially when they're hiring.

For me, when I was hiring I would focus on—and keep using the phrase—the entrepreneurial spirit. The fact that you have autonomy. The fact that if you have an idea that you want to foster and make real, and you can get your day-to-day work done, we have the type of culture that will support that. And we'll help nurture it if we see momentum around it.

"I don't think I would have been where I was in the company if that culture didn't exist. To have a vision for things, and bring them to life; by being able to articulate that in a way using some examples and outcomes, and avoiding the tropes of ping-pong and drinking parties, has been a valuable tool when I was hiring."

The parallel between forming a band and starting a new business sound similar. But what can be learned from the processes and techniques that musicians use within a band to help a business like yours grow? What happens after the first few rehearsals or you're ready to move out of beta?

Now what?

BURNING DOWN THE HOUSE

Unlocking innovation and assessing risk

WHEN A BAND IS together rehearsing and jamming, ideas flow between its members. One person starts to play and the rest of the band quickly (or sometimes not so quickly) picks it up. They start to riff on it over and over. They try an idea because there is trust. And at the very least, they see if the musical idea *works* and *feels right*. And usually within a few minutes, they get a sense if the idea is going on the back burner, getting scrapped completely, or worth working on for the next few hours, days, or weeks.

There is a freedom to take risks and advance the music in this kind of environment. Yes, there can be tension. Yes, there are egos. Big ones. And yes, sometimes there are serious disagreements that cause one of the guitarists to jump across the room and throw a punch or two at the keyboard player. Or maybe that's *just* in one of the bands I played in (though my guess is it's not).

Rapid creation sounds easy to do when the players are right there together and there is a common language to talk an idea out—to see if it moves everyone. And the risk is minimal: you try it and no one dies. The band doesn't break up afterward.

The same holds true for any business. The company doesn't fold if it tries something as a prototype and it doesn't go any further than that. Or you try something out in the market and it doesn't take off as expected.

As Mike Lowenstern explains: "In music you play a wrong note, you play a good note, you play great concerts, you play terrible concerts. It happens in time. And once it's over, it's over. But ultimately, it happens and it's over. Looking at it that way, there's no risk. You can never ever screw up so bad that you can't go and do it right the next time."

Mike goes deeper: "I play a lot of colleges. In fact, that's probably where I play most is at universities and music schools. I will play a concert and it's usually a residency, so the next day I'll go in and talk to classes—give a master class, talk to composers, talk to composition classes, have lunch with people. I ask them to be really open with me, and they are.

"I explain that I'm in advertising, and I'm in marketing, and focus-grouping is part of how I know if I'm successful in that field, so that's how I need to know how I'm successful in this field. And they'll tell me, 'Yeah, this one went on a little bit too long,' or 'I couldn't really hear the words in that one,' or 'I couldn't understand what I think you wanted me to understand.'

"And I'll take that back and I'll look at it. And if it's fixable, I'll fix it, and if it's not, I'll scrap it."

That may be one of the most critical concepts in reframing how we think about risk-taking in business. How many times have you heard business leaders express the need to break things, fail, and learn? Bands do this instinctively in the rehearsal room through jamming and listening. It's instantaneous prototyping. There's no reason you can't emulate jamming in the conference room or out on the floor, regardless of the size of your organization.

I've led team "jam sessions" in companies I've worked at that may start with one person playing a foundational riff like, "We can help marketers connect more meaningfully with people by tailoring a narrative in a video to them using our technology."

Then a *wah-wah* guitar builds on it: "Yes! We have technology that has an understanding of who's looking at a video online and we can map a message for that person. Maybe we can composite that message directly into a video? You know, overlay it somehow?"

(Stay with me.)

Drums come in with a groove: "Love it. I think that's possible technologically speaking, but may be hard to eventually scale using just our own platform. Just sayin'. Any outside companies that can help us?"

A crescendo: "Yep, I know this start-up that's been experimenting with a technology like that but they don't have access to the marketer's content to put into the videos. But *we* do. I can shoot them an email to see if they're up for a quick test with us."

A breakdown to the kick drum: "We'll have to measure the effectiveness of this thing somehow. Gotta prove it works."

Silence.

Everyone comes back in: "We'll absolutely need measurement. But let's see if the thing just *functions* first."

The jam takes shape and begins to peak. Someone takes a lead.

"Perfect. You reach out to that company today to get us on a call to discuss the idea. Send them an NDA. I'll quickly draft up a business case to talk about what we're solving in the market and why this is new and important. I'll run it by a few folks and see what we're not considering. You start thinking really high-level about how this can work architecturally within our stack and operational workflow. Let's aim for a rough outline of this all and meet back in two days and see where we're at."

Jam session done.

When you come back together you may find you have the makings of a "great song": product market fit, some internal buy-in, a client shows interest, the implementation seems doable.

You have to do a quick, rough recording to capture the essence of it: a prototype.

This is a fast process. It's a conversation. It's a whiteboard session. The main concept can move forward or eventually get killed, but you went through the exercise as open-minded as possible and built on ideas to make them better—not tearing down someone's ideas because "they were bad"—until you can step back to see if something is there to work with.

Finding common ground can be tricky when there are various—and strong—personalities, roles, and responsibilities to navigate through.

It's easy to get intimidated or frustrated.

Keeping an open mind and looking at all of the strengths of who's in the room is how new and meaningful ideas originate and ultimately get executed.

Anurag Gulati builds on this: "I was working with mathematicians, or I was working with engineers, or business people that had gone to business school that had learned certain frameworks for success and optimization. I found that everybody had their own core skill set and that what they were doing was reaching into a toolbox of tools that other people had made for them so they could hammer/chisel away at whatever they were trying to get done.

"Sometimes I would think, there are tools that need to be used that don't exist. So if I was to build a tool, what would it be? Approaching something as a blank canvas or an empty recorder is the first and foremost thing that I learned from the music industry.

"The other thing that I learned is improvisation. You know, it's okay to hit a wrong note every now and then because that dissonant sound might take you into a jazz progression that wouldn't have transitioned gracefully there, but now the progression that's occurring is beautiful and seems like it would have been part of the original progression had it not been for that one little 'mess up.'

"Being okay with not getting things one hundred percent correct. Which in my American Express job, I would get something ninety-five percent correct, and they're like, 'We're mathematicians. That five percent matters to us.'

"But I was like, I'm trying out something brand new and trying to be creative about it. The creative process is messy."

Reid talks about the writing process in his former band, Strangefolk, and the process in which songs would take shape:

"Initially we had a few different modes of working together. One was where I'd bring a sketch of a song to the band that basically included the chord progression and lyrics. I think that's the way a lot bands in the era prior to us wrote songs. And everybody wrote their part.

"I would sort of describe, I envision this like a band tune. I hear the part like section of 'Superstition' with a disco groove on it or whatever. Even though that was like, 'here's a tune' more or less, the pieces that I was describing take it from an embryo, or at least from an infant to an adolescent with everybody else's contribution.

"It was often frustrating, too, because— again, this is one of the big lessons I take from this process—people would contribute things that you didn't necessarily envision or like even. And so then the question becomes, 'Do you have the language and interpersonal skills to have them sort of modulate what they're doing to fit your vision?' or 'Can you adjust your vision to include what they've contributed?'

"Sometimes what they did was better than what you had envisioned or even just different. And when I look at what worked for Strangefolk, is that we were unique in what we did because... we were almost defined by our limitations. So instead of being able to cop the 'Superstition' thing exactly, since we couldn't do that, it came out some other way that was uniquely ours."

There is a whole other jam session in actual development of technology. Some people don't realize how incredibly creative the coding process is. At its core, coding is very much built on the concepts of how we communicate and speak to each other; how we anticipate and plan for inputs and responses. You're telling a machine what to do, when to do it, how to do it, and to plan for a complicated set of responses—and perhaps even learn how to anticipate new responses itself.

Programming is proactive problem-solving and iteration of logic to replicate how humans think and behave. Being the most complex creatures on the planet, one would have to be extremely creative in the approach to architecting a piece of technology looking at it this way, right?

Even in that environment, though, you work and learn fast to build upon ideas. I'd posit maybe even more so.

Now take a moment and think about the resources within your business. Whether you have engineers who code or salespeople who create strategic account plans, there are opportunities to test and learn in a similar way with both speed and limited risk. There are ways to start extremely small that will ultimately inform whether or not to go bigger. More importantly, figuring out how to scale this approach across an entire company is what creates a culture of innovation.

Your team is no longer afraid to create something and try it out.

For example, in ad technology it's not unheard of to have a developer work alongside a designer to build a new ad format within a few hours or a day. I've countlessly watched members of a team I used to manage write a few lines of code for a quick "show and tell" of an idea for me; to let me touch and see it first before deciding whether to add more fuel or quickly extinguish it because it didn't line up to a market need (even though it may have looked really, really cool). But the prototype, while taking extreme creativity and thoughtfulness to produce, took little time to build to help visually express the idea.

You may have a strategic sales person on the team who identifies opportunities by examining your product toolkit in new ways. They start with knowing their client's challenges and objectives, then turn to their toolkit to assemble something new and valuable for the client. They put a presentation together to show the client the value of combining the products in this new way.

The product team didn't release anything new, this isn't a scalable solution (yet). But it's real innovation and it's implemented quickly to see if it works or not. I've found that clients are willing to take small risks to learn something new before building on a product or investing more money. But show them you're thinking about them and their business, and building quickly to address their challenges, so everybody wins.

Only after a few small tests happen successfully for a few customers does it make sense to create a roadmap to scale a prototype. I'm not suggesting there aren't elements of your business that shouldn't be viewed through the lens of scale from the start (I have a deep understanding that "custom everything" can get dangerous and unprofitable fast). But no matter the size of the organization, there is always time and at least one resource to try something new.

As Jimmy says: "With the creative process, you always want to keep that paint wet, and always want to be able to change the pigment at any given time."

Cat frames her thoughts on this: "I think that everyone has to come to terms with what it is you're trying to do. And that's why when I said to you that when we play, one of the things we talked about is playing as if you're on the verge of complete and utter destruction. That to us was a good way to say what we're trying to accomplish.

"Whenever we would have a bad practice we'd always go back to that [idea], and nine times out of ten we were let down by ourselves is because we didn't do that. We didn't push ourselves to the point of maybe it all falling apart."

Anurag shares a similar view: "You have to be okay with cleaning up the mess once you get to a certain path. If you put yourself on a structured path and only walk down that line, there's only so much inspiration you can draw from it."

That said, having guardrails and boundaries to work within can often help in evaluating which opportunities to quickly act or pass on.

Glenn Rosenstein elaborates: "In balancing the real needs of the job of being a record producer and running a record label—which was far more a business proposition than a creative proposition—there became this instinctive mental checklist of things where I could assess fairly rapidly where we were wasting time, where we were wasting money. Because efficiency serves creativity just as much, in my humble opinion, as great, creative ideas.

"You can relate to the fact that if we're sitting around and beating the same part over and over and over, that your inspiration is going to go out the window after three or four takes. And if we're on take three hundred, and we've spent twelve hours getting two bars of guitar parts, that's not only an inefficient way of working financially, but an inefficient way of working creatively."

Ultimately you have to either build on ideas, kill them, or pivot.

But you have to keep moving forward no matter what. And often times the only way to learn how to do that—as Jimmy perfectly sums up—is "just by burning the house down."

It's often that innovation comes from pulling together and bridging unexpected ideas, products, solutions, etc. into something new and valuable.

Jimmy continues, showing how bringing disparate elements together can make something different and exciting: "I was talking to a friend of mine yesterday who's an excellent jazz bass player. He plays upright bass with Herbie Hancock. He's a songwriting partner of mine. He's been one of my best friends for over twenty years now. And we were talking about the song, 'Tonight, Tonight.'

"He said, 'How did that song come about?'

"I was telling him the story of the song. And this is an example of confidence and just putting the work in. To the best of my recollection, I think [Billy] Corgan woke up one morning and the song had just come to him in its entirety. He went down to the piano and he played the song. He came to practice that day and he had the entire song written.

"The first time I heard it, I immediately recognized things I had been trying to do on the drum set. I brought in two drum patterns, both for the verse and then the chorus. And they were just born out of the fact that I possessed knowledge about other types of music.

"So when my friend asks, 'Well, how did you come up with drum part,' I said, 'If you listen closely, the clave high-hat part is really taken from the *Heavy Weather*, Weather Report album. The drum track that Alex Acuna plays in "Birdland" is exactly the same part.'

"And he goes, 'Fuck, I never even thought of that. That is so crazy. I've heard "Birdland" and played "Birdland" ten thousand times. But I never put two and two together that that part was taken from that song.'

"And he says, 'Now that you tell me that, it makes total sense.'

"And I told him where the other part came from. The impetus of it, the emotional part, came from this old Gino Vannelli record, where Graham Lear plays this incredible militaristic drum part over this whole side of a record suite.

"And I said it's not the drum part, but the intent is very similar. And I was looking for that type of intent. And that's how that whole marching chorus thing came about.

"But that's a great example of where having that knowledge—that it's so simple when you explain it to people, but it's really born of just years and years of listening and keeping it in your back pocket for that perfect moment when it comes out. And you just lay it out.

"I think there's ton of those examples in business to where you'll see someone has a past in something completely, seemingly irrelevant to what they're doing today. But some of that information will reveal itself in a completely culture-changing feature.

"I mean look at Twitter. Twitter is a great example of a WordPress site turned into something that's completely culturally relevant. That would have never been born if Evan

Williams wasn't doing WordPress. Which in and of itself seems completely mundane and boring. But once you force that as a concept into a small box, it becomes like super-dynamite, right? Once you're forced to distill *Finnegans Wake* down into one hundred and forty characters, all of a sudden it becomes super compelling.

"Those are the types of things that I look for in business that are very representative and reminiscent of the kind of things that I've experienced as a musician."

Prototyping with minimal risk and investment is one thing. But how do you know when to put more into an idea? What are the things to look for? And are there parallels to draw from the music business?

Glenn feels this may be one place these two worlds diverge a bit: "In M&A, the space we occupy—I don't do much in the way of private equity. And private equity would probably be much more related to music production than M&A would. M&A is looking for profitable businesses in search of financial partners, looking to sell, or looking to acquire other business. Private equity is a bit more entrepreneurial. They look at something that may be a risk. It might be a start-up, it may be a need of angel investing, it may be early phase. I did that at Maxim Group, but I don't do that currently. That's not my job now.

"That said, there are these businesses that are profitable, that are "small" profitable. The analogy would be parallel to an indie band that is not signed to a major label. They are making *some* money—I hate breaking it all down to finance, but we are making that comparison. There are businesses that I see that may not fit our profile, but I still have deep interest in seeing them succeed because I feel the same sense of passion that the owners of that business, and the talent of that business, have for what they consider to be their mission. The same as I would see in a young band that's doing self-released music. And is doing not necessarily formidable business, but is doing enough of it on their own: selling merch, distributing their product independently, having a website, doing stuff through social media. I see those parallels. In the business side we are looking for passionate businesses, we are looking for individuals who are as convinced that their product or service is the next best thing for mankind, as any artist would feel that their song is a smash hit. Their playing ability is something that needs to be heard. We love that, don't we? Isn't that *why* we do this?

"That is the crux of what I'm trying to say. The thing that makes me feel good about moving from one world to the other, and for that matter *back*—I still do both—is that it's really about passion.

"It's passion tied to experience, tied to the ability to create something of value. Not necessarily financial value, but there has to be value. Because the vast majority of people are incapable of making some sort of Mozart or Beatles statement in their lifetime. And the same thing with business. If you find *something*, and you find *someone* capable of doing that, of course you want to throw resources behind that—because that *is* the reason we do this. We love finding that passion. We love finding that talent. And then we want to be attached to it. We want to be, in some small way, helpful. It's to be a cog in a bigger wheel that creates something that serves people. From the artistic aesthetic or it's some invention that revolutionizes the way that people interact with each other. All of these things are higher-purpose driven."

Sometimes, it's just not the right moment to try something new. You need to know what the right time and place for it is. I asked Naomi Margolin to think through how she knows when those moments are.

She laughs and says: "It depends whether I'm the star or not. If I'm not the star, that's not the time to do it. It may be the time in a rehearsal, right? To see if everyone's comfortable with it and everybody's gonna remember it. I remember we were doing the first Obama inauguration. We did one of the balls for the Creative Coalition. We were doing a song that had some cool background vocal parts. Some of them are anticipated, and some of them aren't. It mixes it up a lot in the song and that's part of why it's so interesting. And it's not like you have days of rehearsals. You show up at the gig, you do a soundcheck, and in between the soundcheck and the gig is the time you break off into a section and you get to rehearse all the tunes you're doing because you just got the list at sound check. So everyone's got like one earbud in their ear with their phones listening, mapping it to get it get it right.

"Again, with business, you can make all the business plans you want. But you walk into the meeting and they're like, 'we're not interested in buying this, we want *this*,' you gotta be prepared for it. So we're sitting there saying, 'Okay this part is anticipated and this part isn't. And the next one's not and the next one is.' And we realize that with the other eleven songs we're learning just at that moment: we're gonna screw it up.

"We all have to be on the same page, and some of the guys in the band are gonna be singing, too. It's not just about how slick it will sound if *we* get it right 'cause we got *them*, too. It's too much."

So Naomi and her vocal section talked it through together, the clock ticking down to their performance.

"'Okay, let's just make a decision. Either we're going to anticipate all of them or we're gonna sing them all straight.' Again, it wasn't about being slick. It was about how do we get it to sound like we're doing this together.

"So that wasn't a time to experiment. We rehearsed it. We talked it through. And not the time."

This may come down to your gut and an understanding of the urgency of missing the opportunity. And understanding the opportunity in the first place. But let me be clear: don't mistake lack of trying for fear of failing. If you don't try, you don't get to fail or learn or win. The only thing that happens is you have a great idea you don't create and it goes to someone else. Maybe your competitor.

Let's flip the record over and switch things up a little.

I've written songs where I know exactly how I'd like it to sound. I can hear the orchestration. I can even "see" it. The process typically begins with just my guitar and my voice to create the "core song" from which everything else can support and make bigger.

Have you ever listened to a song from an album and it moves you so deeply, and you know every moment of the song—when the singer's voice cracks slightly, or that special guitar or piano lick that you mimic in the air, or the drum part you play on your desk—it's so intimately known. I know "Something" by The Beatles inside and out. Every drum fill, every slight delay when Harrison approaches one of the chromatic guitar licks, the laid-back-yet-earnest delivery in his voice. The version on *Abbey Road* is etched in millions of minds and hearts around the world.

But I feel some of the best songs are translatable to other versions. You still hear the brilliance. Maybe even more so.

Maybe it's an acoustic version. Maybe it's a very raw live version. Maybe another artist covers it. While different from the original version, it still moves you. Maybe even more or in a different way.

When you're building new products, when you're thinking of new business ideas: is the idea so good and powerful that it's something another business would "cover" and try to make their own?

Is the product so meaningful and useful that it doesn't matter if people are engaging with it from their phone, their computer, their car, or their refrigerator?

Is there a *core* to the idea? A source of truth and meaning? So if another company embraced it in their own products, its origins could easily be traced be back to yours?

A fair question here is: Does that really matter? What if you're *at* the company that's building and enhancing someone else's ideas? Does it make what you release to the world less important or useful? Does it make it less innovative?

Of course not.

Let me be clear. My observations here are not about the value in the *origins* of ideas, but rather the *quality* of them. How do you even define quality in this instance? And one step beyond that: can you execute flawlessly once you commit to seeing an idea become real, then deliver the quality of experience you promised to the people who will use what you're producing?

Don't answer that yet.

Let's bring it back down now and come back to the main concept before moving ahead.

Be kind and open when you're brainstorming. Build on ideas, don't tear them down. When you're done, figure out which ideas fit best with what you're trying to solve and then

just try it.

Small first. One client. Test, learn, stop or continue. If you stop, great. If you continue, great. What's next?

And remember that if you play one or two wrong notes, the crowd won't leave. They already knew you were taking a chance and trying to create something new *for them*. They're on your side because you set that expectation up front.

Thinking like this:

what will you try next?

Businesses

typically don't

operate well if

there isn't mutual

respect

COME TOGETHER

Building bridges, establishing credibility, and building strong partnerships internally and externally

#SpoilerAlert

BUSINESSES TYPICALLY DON'T OPERATE well if there isn't mutual respect, trust, and ground rules for an open flow of communication to share ideas. That culture has to be established from the start and embodied by the leadership and everyone in the organization. Whether that's done as part of the on-boarding process for new hires, at every all-hands meeting for a quarterly update, or stated at the beginning of each meeting—everyone needs to tune themselves up before trying to play a song together, and get themselves familiar with the material beforehand.

Al talks about this at the genesis of forming moe.: "You're putting your own sense of self out there to be—again, just by creating the band—

you're putting it in the hands of these other guys and saying, 'Okay, here you go. I'm trusting you with this. Please, don't hurt me.' At the same time, in the best interest of the band, we all need to be critical and fair, and you hope that whatever it is you're creating comes out to be the best version of that for the band."

Anurag helps explain further: "In order for me to give input to an artist, who is usually protective of their craft, I have to build a rapport, build a bridge, and a mutual understanding and respect. That's what I had to do before I could start pushing on, 'Hey, change this, or try that.'

"I feel like I bring the same thing to business. Especially because I'm in partnerships where I do business development. First I have to go talk with potential partners, have them understand me as a person, have them respect me and what my capabilities are, and then agree on mutual goals. Whether that's making the track sound amazing or building a partnership between two companies. If we both share the same goal and we have that mutual respect, then we can really start building the bridge to where we can be collaborative and start pushing things forward."

Imagine being in a not-so-clean (or even operational) van for four weeks heading across the United States with four other people. Tight quarters, little money, awful smells. You're praying that enough people show up to the gig in Iowa City tonight to make enough money for food and gas to get to St. Louis tomorrow. And even if five hundred people show up, you hope the booking agent at the club doesn't stiff you. There's a certain amount of resilience needed for this career—and for your fellow bandmates—that is required to persist and continue on. And more times than not, what keeps you all going is the dedication to the vision that brought you together in the first place.

Reid reflects on this: "The thing related to that is that the ability to orchestrate different people with different skill sets, different personalities, around that common vision is also central. It's made me a tolerant boss, a tolerant coworker, a tolerant employee, in that I just saw the complexity of that at a really young age. And out of sheer will, was able to navigate through it. And to do so with incredible amounts of pressure and responsibility."

Rob shares a similar perspective: "I think I learned that by working together on songwriting, and the whole group being better than the individual. But it's not just songwriting. It's marketing, it's everything. From a simple T-shirt design, you're gonna get the guy that's not the 'creative guy' that's going to give you one idea or critique that then blossoms into something else."

The whole concept of collaboration, open brainstorming, and working together is really translatable.

Rob continues: "I think the entrepreneurial spirit of the DIY scene is something that has carried me this entire time. It's this 'get shit done' attitude. But it's doing it in a way that is respectful of the community. It's not that I'm an island and I'm going to plow through this work and 'fuck everything else.'

"It's really building relationships and building consensus. We'd be sitting in brainstorming sessions and somebody would come up with something. It would be off the wall, not fit, and you'd hear a lot of the folks immediately start to shut it down. It's like someone saying, 'We're doing this thing in five–four time, and the guitar solo is in three–four. How is this going to fit in?' It's making sure you don't kill an idea before it's even started to blossom. You see it through first. Sometimes it works, sometimes it doesn't. But being open to new things, new ideas, and not taking the path of least resistance—and being collaborative—is definitely translated."

When the idea of trust comes up with Cat, she echoes this:

> *When you're truly doing a good creative partnership you know what the role is and where your lines are.*

"You have to have enough freedom of creation and trust with the people that you're working with that you can go beyond the defined role you play. But you have to know when you've crossed into someone else's territory so that they have the freedom to create, too.

"That's the partnership I have with the creative directors that [I] work with. I bring ideas to the table. And probably if I was in a smaller agency, I could come up with the concepts and they'd be good. But they're not as good as when I work with a really great creative partner, just like my songs aren't as good if I just do them on my own."

What are you doing to build trust within your company? What about with your clients and partners? What's one thing different you can try tomorrow to show you have empathy for your colleagues?

GOT TO BE REAL

Authenticity

WHETHER A BUSINESS JUST got off the ground after some seed money or has been around for over a hundred years, presenting a consistent and authentic brand voice to customers can be one of the biggest challenges to overcome.

Do people believe you? Do you sound like a person or a robot? Is there trust and connection?

Cat talks about a few brands and musical artists she sees keeping true to their selves:

"Younger brands tend to have an easier time doing it because they remember their founding principles. So I think Warby Parker is a good one. Uber is a good one. AirBnB. I think Virgin as a whole portfolio of brands is very much that, but it's partly because their founder is still so greatly involved. He himself is a walking brief. So you know they're going to continue to do things in their own way.

"Once you get, as a company, to a place where you're no longer the challenger, and you're trying to become more mainstream, that's when most brands begin to lose their way because they think they have to change in order to grow to the next generation. And often times, all that's required is to be true to yourself, but allow for how that's expressed to change and be more relevant given the times or the people you want to engage.

"And I think that's true for music, too.

"So Nick Cave hasn't—it's not like there is a cliché Nick Cave album. He's changed over the course of time, but he's always remained true to something that's in him, and I think that's part of what makes both a musician and a brand successful—it doesn't mean being a cliché, it doesn't mean doing it the same way you've always done. It's basically understanding why you are doing it, and how that might impact people, so that what you do ends up being slightly different, but the *how* and the *why* doesn't necessarily change."

How can leaders establish trust and unity with their teams and peers? How can business leaders learn what's working and not working much sooner?

Listen up.

*What are the things that **make me unique** in the business world?*

WHAT ARE YOU LISTENING TO?

The power of listening

#Flashback

I GET THIS CALL from our cellist/piano player that our band was asked to play a benefit for a member of the great Colorado jam band, Leftover Salmon, who was fighting cancer. We were already in the van headed to NYC before there was even time to discuss.

Besides us doing a good thing for a good person, I didn't expect I was about to get a major life lesson that night.

We roll into B. B. King's in Times Square and it turns out there were few other folks from the scene who were also performing that night. There were two, in particular, that I was a bit awe-struck by: John Medeski of Medeski Martin and Wood, and Mike Gordon from Phish.

We play our set. Medeski plays a set. Gordon plays a set. And then at the end of the night, this open jam emerges and I find myself on stage with both of them. John starts playing an incredible chunky riff on the B3, Mike comes in with a melodic thump along with the drummer who's laying down a simple, solid groove. And then there's me: the overly excited, need-to-prove-myself-to-these-guys guitar player.

I knew what I was going to play before I even picked up my guitar. So I start to play what I believe is a really great single-note riff, ala The Meters, moments after the jam starts. Maybe four bars go by when I get a look from Mike Gordon.

Let me tell you. In all of my years on earth I have never felt the coldness of a stare from anyone as intense as the one I got from Mike Gordon after I started playing. I was confused, crushed, and silenced.

I was tempted to put the guitar down and walk off the stage. I thought, *I'm done.*

And then something happened: I just listened. I listened harder than I ever listened before as a musician to everything that was happening around me. And I had to decide what would be best to contribute to the music, not "what would sound cool from the guitar player."

I opened my ears, took a breath, and eventually landed on a very sparse, mid-register diatonic hammer-on riff. I played it soft to make sure it blended with the musical moment we were in. And I really felt it did fit there; that it sounded like it had always belonged there even though it was improvised.

I slowly turned my head to look at Gordon— and god, I was scared to make any eye contact— but I needed to get a visual read from him. And he smiled a quick smile to let me know I got it.

Lesson learned.

How well do *you* listen?

Flat out: how well do you know your customers and are you listening to them and anticipating their needs?

How well do you know their behaviors, their expectations, their mindset in various contexts? How well do you know your customer's customers? Have you asked them directly, really opened up and listened, prepared that everything you expect to hear may be the complete opposite of what you thought?

In what way does your product or services fit into their world? How often does it make its way into their day or week? What triggers them to think about it?

Reid talks about the criticality of knowing and listening to your audience: "The one thing I think is central to any business—and I think musicians have an unfair advantage on understanding—is this notion of product market fit. You know as an artist when you've got something that's resonating with people. On a macro scale, if it's gaining steam and you're feeling momentum and you're seeing momentum in your ticket sales, and your merch sales, and that kind of stuff—and then on a micro level when you're songwriting and you play a new song and you see whether or not the crowd responds to it. You know almost instantly if there's something there."

Al agrees that it all comes down to listening to the audience: "Because so much of what we do, especially while improvising, is feeding off of the energy of our audience. There's a very real exchange between getting some immediate feedback on what we're doing. Yes, this works. This is bad. Are we losing the audience, do we have them?

"It's so important to what we do.

If we're not listening to our audience then we're just doing this for ourselves.

We might as well be back in a basement in Buffalo."

Mike connects listening directly to successful marketing: "If you're in a coffee shop, or rather you're in a restaurant, you are not playing loud because that's not what the behavior is and the expectation is of you. You are playing quietly and you are background music. Period. You're not strolling around, you're not engaging the customers, you are not interrupting people. You're just background music.

Then when you're on the stage at a concert-concert, and people are there to come and see you, and that's your focus—that's something different. But you have to understand what the expectation and the behavior of your audience is.

That's primary for everything that we do, understanding the medium if you will, the placement."

Sounds like a simple and effective approach, right?

And if you're still unsure, maybe Jimmy will convince you: "I think it's: know thyself and know thy audience.

"It's the biggest thing. If you look at Steve Jobs—and I'm not a huge Steve Jobs disciple. I'm more like in the Ben Horowitz, Peter Thiel camp. But if you look at the companies historically that have been uber successful, they've had incredible product market fit and they've known things that other people haven't.

"Thiel does a great job of explaining this in a very nuts and bolts way in his book. But to take it one step further: what are the concepts that you as a business or a business leader can monopolize?

What are the things that you know that nobody else knows?

"And if you take those things, can you make them into products? Can you make those into philosophies? Can you make them into business strategies that give you that leg up?

"I think often times, business leaders make assumptions—or they don't make assumptions—about the knowledge they possess and they don't capitalize on it.

"Just for me, when I joined LiveOne there were things I knew about content consumption that very few fucking people could know. Cause I'm one of a hundred people that have ever headlined the Reading Festival. I'm one of maybe ten business leaders—or maybe even less—that have headlined Lollapalooza or played in front of ninety-thousand people.

"So when I look at those things as a value prop for my company, I try to monopolize those concepts as much as I can: what are the things that make me unique in the business world? What are the things that I know? What's the knowledge that I possess from both a content creator and a content consumer that gives me credibility and an ability to produce those records—to my previous comments—beyond what people think they're capable of?

"That's where I see the most missteps. And I'm not proclaiming to be some business guru. I'm only speaking from what I know personally, and the only things that have helped me be a business leader. And the only things that have given me the confidence to move forward.

"Because when I speak about standing on stage, and the way the environment plays into that experience, I know what the fuck I'm talking about. You can't take that away from me. And very few people could anyway because they haven't experienced it. So those are the types of things that, as a business leader, I can kind of monopolize as a concept and move forward.

"And when I look around in a room of people, every one of those people has knowledge that only they possess, right? Those are the things that I think businesses need to key more in on. As opposed to this Eric Ries, lean start-up methodology. Which works on a business principle. But once you start applying that to the creative process it kind of collapses under its own weight."

Now: how well are you listening to your team and your peers?

Listening to each other usually comes with the territory of a successful band. Or at least a band that connects deeply with people.

Without listening, things just don't feel or sound right.

Just as important is having an awareness that you alone don't need to have all of the answers. It's possibly one of the most liberating and useful pieces of information to lean on within a business setting during challenging moments.

Jimmy talks about what can happen when you try to go it alone both in a band and in business: "When I left the Pumpkins in '09, Billy was kind of left without a sounding board. He was just having to make decisions solely on his own. Which I think anybody who is left to their own devices, that becomes a very murky place to live.

"Certainly when you have a band, it gets harder to move things around, and it becomes more of a process. And sometimes becomes more of a pain in the ass than it's worth. So therefore, the band sustains its brand and its identity by the nature of: it's too much work to change it.

"But when you get into a larger company like LiveOne, then it becomes more important not to dictate, but to listen. And to make sure that I'm not missing important parts of our identity that may go overlooked if it's just my version.

"So for me, it's being more like a jazz musician. When you're in a rock band, in a quartet, it's kind of one thing, but when you get into a big band or a symphony, it becomes more important to listen and be compassionate to what you're hearing, and try to fit that into the ideal of the company, rather than to dictate.

"And I've tried both. And I've had meetings where I'm like, 'Okay, this is what we're going to do.' And I've had meetings that are like, 'What are we going to do?'

"I think depending on the circumstances, often times ask, 'What are we going to do?' even if you *know* what you're going to do…

"Let's say I know that no matter what everybody says, I know what I'm going to do. It's still important for me to ask the question, 'What are we going to do?' because you never know. Sometimes you figure out what you're going to do, and then you find out that everybody wants to do exactly what you want to do. But every once in a while you figure out what you want to do, and you figure out that ninety percent of the people think that's a dumb idea, and you're forced to go back and reexamine.

"And maybe you don't let that cat out of the bag, but it's certainly important for the success of a business to be knowledgeable. Especially for a company like LiveOne. I mean, I'm fifty-one years old. So, for me, social media means something totally different than it does to my twenty-one-year-old employee. So, for me, to have any type of cultural product market fit, I've gotta know if things are cool or not, right? Because I'm showing up in my old man jeans and my Versace shirt—I mean, who *knows* what I'm pulling out of *my* closet. I mean, some of the stuff is ten, twenty years old. My employees could be looking at me in complete horror, going, 'That guy is going to lead our product development?'

"As cool as I may think I am, I've got to be cognizant of the fact that I may not be *that* cool. At least have a knowledge of where that culture needs to go, or be driven to, in order to be successful."

Understanding your audience and customers is one component here, and learning to "let go" in different business situations is another thing and can be extremely challenging—but rewarding.

Adapting quickly to change is critical because most things are out of your control.

Touring musicians run into unexpected situations every day that affect business: van breaks down, no promotion when you roll into town, promoter tries to stiff you, or someone starts a fight during your show. And somehow the band still gets to the venue with all their gear (thank you, fellow travelers of the road), they quickly make a few more posts about your show to let more people know you're in town (thank you, social media), they fast-talk, referencing their agreement to get paid to cover gas and food (thank you bass player who keeps all the emails organized on his phone), and they have a tour manager who doesn't actually have a black belt to protect everyone, but is one hell of an actor.

What comes up in your day-to-day? Have you gotten so familiar with the types of situations that can arise that you have your own playbook for responding to them? It becomes second-nature.

Listening and reacting.
Observing and responding.

You're familiar with the call-and-response in music, right?

When I say, "Hey!" you say "Ho!"

Hey! (Ho!)

You listen for the call and you respond. And it just feels right when you do it. Why can't your relationship with your customers and colleagues replicate this? With interactions like these, you'd think you were performing, right? Well maybe you are.

Even if you're not in control of a situation,

good things can come from it

WELCOME BACK MY FRIENDS, TO THE SHOW THAT NEVER ENDS

Performing isn't just for bands and artists

THE STAGE. THE AUDIENCE. THE PERFORMANCE.

Rock concert or client pitch?

When Mike brings his team to a client pitch, he doesn't see much difference at all: "What you're doing is performing and you have to know who you're performing to. They [my team] get it. None of them are musicians, actually. But they all understand it.

"Any time I'm in a pitch, anytime I'm in a presentation and I'm selling something, it is me on the stage giving a concert. And the weird thing is that I get the same rush after we leave. On the elevator down I'm like, 'Hey, let's go get a beer!' I get the same rush out of it.

"But really, you're reading a room. And some rooms are hard to read. I know you know this. Where they just don't want to be there, where something is just off. It's usually not you. Because if you're a good a performer, everyone will at least appreciate the fact that you're a good performer. And, again, when I say performer, I'm talking about in a pitch setting. They'll recognize your craft. They may not like what you're doing, but they recognize that you're doing it well. Because there's too many presentations that are just droning on and on and on."

Get off the sheet music and perform.

There is just as much rehearsing required to perfect the craft of connecting with people in a conference room as there is at a club or stadium. Don't underestimate the importance of rehearsing and owning the material.

I'm not suggesting you have to be extremely charismatic or an extrovert to break through to a live audience. But I am positing that if you can't communicate well to any size room and adjust to the reaction of the people as your presentation progresses, then you're missing a big opportunity to inspire them to act. Whether that room is filled with your team, your partners, or your clients. With enough practice, you learn to respond faster and more appropriately. You learn to improvise because you're comfortable enough with the material to do so.

Cat talks about how years of performing on stage prepares her for meetings: "I think that what performing and going on the road in general does is that you learn to give up control. You always learn that even if you're not in control of a situation that good things can come from it. When you're on the road—I can't tell you the number of times that we've shown up at a club and it's either smaller than you think, or the sound isn't what you hoped for, or you don't have a sound check before you go on.

> *I think that's a pretty important thing: being ready for anything.*

"Even today, I can't tell you the number of times I've showed up for a client meeting or a business engagement and I had one set of expectations for what my role was supposed to be. Or what the meeting was about. And I've been put in a position where I have to perform instead of participate, and I can do that without any problem. And that ability to perform at any moment, I think that truly does come from an understanding that there are situations that you're not going to be in control of; the unexpected will come all the time and it will still be okay."

When asked more about the physical energy put into presenting to clients compared to performing a rock show on stage, Cat agrees that everything has to go into it: "We have this joke that we're on the verge of complete and utter destruction. It's the way we play our set. We're always right on the edge of everything going to hell. [We] try to put ourselves out there as much as possible.

"And at the end of our set, I'm physically beat. My body hurts the next day 'cause we give it everything whenever we perform."

And does the same energy translate to a pitch in the boardroom? Cat says yes.

"You have to because to me strategy is just a narrative journey, and songs are a narrative journey. Are you telling the best story you can tell? Have you gotten people from the beginning, brought them through the arc of a story, and come to some kind of resolution? And a pitch is just that: just one elaborate story.

"It's the same thing. You have to orchestrate the roles, you have to play people to their strengths, and you have to bring the people who are in the audience at a pitch on a journey that hopefully will get them to think differently about either your agency, your ideas that you're putting on the table, or even what they can be as a brand."

That's really the purpose. You're supposed to bring people on a journey.

Continue to push the envelope

WHO ARE YOU?

Defining roles and getting the best out of your team

I'M NOT THAT SMART. I mean, I consider myself somewhat intelligent, but there are people I work with that are literally geniuses. I feel very lucky to be surrounded by people way, way smarter than I am. And not only lucky, but very comfortable with my role and the strengths I contribute to my team, my company, and my partners.

The roles within bands can take shape pretty quickly when they form. For example, the guitarist and keyboardist may write the music, the singer writes the lyrics and melody, the drummer helps in arrangement, and the bass player is responsible for: accounting, booking the band, marketing, managing the email list, and making sure the club provides a sufficient amount of Pabsts backstage.

I kid, but not really.

Everyone plays a part. Everyone contributes. Some more than others.

When talking about the roles within moe., Al says they're not only established after twenty-five years, but emphasizes again the importance of culture and fit to support everyone's role in the band: "The musical dynamic I guess that we have as a band—in terms of the roles we play musically, on stage, during improvisation, or otherwise—that dynamic is not a whole lot different than the roles we also maintain during a business meeting, or an email thread about figuring tour plans, merchandise ideas, whatever the thing may be. But it always tends to be the same. Which is sort of interesting.

"For example, [moe. drummer] Vinnie [Amico] is an amazing drummer. And we can count on him to be there and be a great, stable rhythm player for us with good ideas that augment whatever it is that we're already doing. But even in the context of our music, it's very rare that Vinnie will come up with an idea on his own. Vinnie has essentially written one song with moe. It's very unusual for him to start a musical idea even in the context of improvising on stage.

"That's not to say he's devoid of creativity or ideas, because like I said, a lot of what he does are subtle changes within the flow of what's already happening. I would say the same thing happens within the context of our business, too. Vinnie tends to be very agreeable and might offer little tweaks to ideas, but he's not going to start a meeting, he's not going to come to the table with, 'Hey guys, we need to sit down and talk because I've been thinking about this and want to come up with a new way that we should we start touring.'

"Know what I mean? His role both onstage and offstage are very comparable.

"I would say that's probably true of all of us.

"As you probably imagine, [moe. bass guitarist] Rob [Derhak] plays a very dominant role in both cases. That's just the way it goes. Everybody's roles are very similar. I don't know if that's because we are who we are, whether we have instruments in our hands or laptops in our hands.

"The funny thing is, if it's a day off and we're all going to the movies or going out to dinner together, the roles are pretty much the same.

"I don't see any radical shifts coming. Every now and then someone will surprise you. But you know, we're old men and we've been doing this together for twenty-five years. And like you said, it's like people who have been hanging out together for a long time. It sort of makes you think of the cast of *Seinfeld*, or something. Everybody kind of is their own character.

"But we are who we are. And it doesn't make a difference if we're on stage or having a meeting or hanging out together. We're still who we are in those personalities, and that group dynamic sorta prevails no matter what the context.

"And I go back to that thing, all being able to get along somehow which is why I think it works somehow. It's been important to us that it crosses over to our crew and the people in the home office, because we've had crew members who are extremely talented at their jobs but didn't fit in dynamically into the group. And that became a problem over time. And, unfortunately, we'd end up parting ways. That person would quit or we would have to let them go. It was always important for us first and foremost that you could 'ride the bus.'

"You gotta be able to be on the bus and get along with everyone and hang out with us.

And then hopefully you're really good at your job, too. [*Laughs*]"

As business leaders, sometimes the best thing you can do in your role is just get out of the way.

Let someone else take the lead.

In music, it's not just the rhythm guitarist, or the piano player, backing up the guitarist on a solo, even though they all can shred. It's also the saxophone player in a jazz quartet laying out so the rhythm section can trade fours. It's everybody leaving the stage for a bass solo. (Ever notice the audience gets especially fired up when this happens?)

What leaders need to be able to do is simply be comfortable playing a supporting role. Naomi talks through this, "Often, my client needs additional expertise beyond what I do to be able to close the deal with his client. So my client is the middle-man in the sale. He's selling my product to somebody else. You have to earn that trust. If somebody is going to put you in front of their client, they have to trust you. And [the] philosophy that I find I voice often in those settings is that my job when we go out together is not to be the star. Just like that first gig with Sam Moore. My job is to not fuck it up, to support you, to distract the audience if you need a minute, and to make you smarter and to make you better.

To make you the star.

"And being able to articulate that to somebody puts them at ease. It may not be a conversation they're used to having before. But letting them know that not only am I aware of what they're concern is, but I've been mastering that and working the craft of it for decades, makes it easier for them to understand that I get it. I get it. I know my place, I know what I'm going to do, and I'm not looking to be that star."

Defining the roles within a company should help set expectations for both the person filling the role and their peers in knowing how and when to engage with them. Many times role descriptions are left vague and obtuse, which can cause confusion and territorial conflicts with someone who believes they're responsible for something they're not.

Glenn tells a great story about starting out as a receptionist at New York's famed recording studio, Power Station, and ultimately becoming a record producer: "I learned more about the music industry, and about being a record producer and a business person by answering telephones in the middle of the night, and scoring drugs, and taking in people's laundry, and dropping people off, and parking cars. I learned an enormous amount about what it means to be servile.

"That boded very well long-term. And that's actually how I got my start in the business. I did spend some time on the road post-college doing live sound, so there was a good education component prior to walking into the studio. But once I got into Power Station [there] was a strong mentorship program that was very informal. It wasn't part of my employ there. But I had guys like Bob Clearmountain, Neil Dorfsman, and Scott Litt. At the time, real stars.

"And they'd be like, 'Hey, Glenn, go put the phone on night answer, come in, don't say a fucking word. Watch what we do, don't say anything, don't ask any questions.'

Just experience it.

"And it was awesome. It jump-started in me a real option and a real possibility to be working with world-class engineers and world-class musicians on records. And at least at that the time, that mattered.

"Even if it was on a very subtle level, very nonparticipatory level initially because I was learning, it still taught me about what that process looked like.

"Fundamentally from the outset, I didn't understand what the job definition was. I didn't go to a school for it, there was nothing really written in stone when I was getting started. So I think from the beginning—from high school and even in any bands I was in—I always had an opinion. And whether or not it was appreciated [*laughs*] or accepted, I always had a strong opinion about the way I thought music should sound

"I didn't really know what a producer *did*. But, gradually, I found out. As an assistant engineer, I would study the relationship between the producer and the engineer. And as an assistant engineer, gosh, I worked on albums for David Bowie, Bruce Springsteen, and The Cars.

And I would get a sense that—again, finances absolutely aside because we both know that back in those days producers were wealthy if they had hits, and engineers were not—I was intrigued with the idea of having a more specific musical rather than technological influence on the interactions that were going on in the studio. So, clearly, very early on, it was defined for me that production was more the direction that I wanted to go.

"In either case, it was a very, very hard gig to get. People don't hand those gigs out. You have to be extraordinarily lucky, you have to be very much in the right place at the right time. I think that working at Power Station was a great 'right-place-at-the-right-time' thing. It was just a place where music was being made, and a lot of amazing, fairly-well-known talents—and not only musical talents. I'm talking about producers, attorneys, and managers, congregated. It was a great, a great cocktail party to be at."

Jimmy also talks about roles of the Pumpkins and how important they are to creating boundaries of play and defining the band: "I think there's a lot of assumptions around the Pumpkins, just by nature of the fact it's pretty common knowledge now that Billy and I made all the records together. We played all the instruments ourselves. And James [Iha] and D'arcy [Wretzky] really didn't play on the records. But their contribution, nevertheless—at least in my opinion—was completely vital to the organization in that James was really interested in this kind of country rock type of music, that Billy and I took a look at and kind of mined some information out of.

"D'arcy, from a cultural standpoint, was very connected. So she was the person in the band that made sure we weren't geeking out too much and that we always stayed kinda cool. And, obviously, Billy's role was the chief songwriter. But my job in the band was really arrangements, and trimming the fat out of songs, and making sure that we weren't just stroking each other for the sake of self-indulgence. And, also, pushing everyone as a musician.

"'Cause I'm, still to this day, just a staunch advocate of practicing everyday. I'm always practicing and always trying to evolve on the instrument. So I think that in a lot of ways, I scared Corgan to the point where he was forced to practice all the time and continually up his game. Because when we would show up to rehearsal it would be like, 'Okay, man, don't play what you played last week. Let's see what you got now. What have you been working on?' So if you weren't working on stuff, it was immediately exposed if you were delivering the same old hash.

"And even to this day, I just did a tour with the Pumpkins and I think they weren't surprised to know that I had gone on to make two successful jazz bebop records, both of which charted very highly. And I've taken on this whole new musical personal, in jazz and bebop and fusion. But continue to push the envelope.

"That was kind of my role. And keeping the band accountable to having a destination. I'm a really big believer in the universe, and letting things happen, and making yourself available for guidance. But I'm also a big believer in strategy and having a reason for being. I'm not a big fan of, 'Hey, let's get in a room and see what happens.' I'm more of a fan of..."

Here's the destination. Let's figure out how to get there.

Finding new talent to fill roles within a company bears a striking similarity to the job of a record producer. Glenn explains: "As a producer, I am a casting director. I find the right musicians if it is a single artist, or the right ringers if the guys in the band don't play on their own records, the right engineer, the right studio, the right location.

"I see that same experience in being a casting director. I'm not an HR person, but clearly because we're a small firm and a lot of strength lies in interactions with our brokers, everybody that we interact with becomes a very important piece of each transaction. We do see very early on, from the instinct that I developed in the music business, whether these people are capable of embracing the vision that we have. And that they share the passion that we have for our business in a meaningful way.

"So I hire a drummer to play on an album because the drummer was unable to play, something happened. And that person was not of the same mindset, of the same team, for lack of a better word, the same vibe—that project would not go very well and would likely fail.

And everybody would go, 'You know, Glenn. We're not blaming you for the guy's ability. But you thought he'd be a great fit.'

"It might be unspoken, but that would be there.

"So you are always carefully vetting who the right player is.

Your team is paramount to the skill-set that you bring to the game.

"Very much the same thing in the financial world. It's very easy because of the years of experience I have to tell fairly quickly whether somebody is going to be a real resource for us, and hence a real resource for themselves. They'll profit remarkably by being a great team player. If they are not, it's not going to be just a waste of our time, even more importantly, it'll be a waste of *their* time. They're not going to achieve the goals that they had and the things that they wanted to do.

"It's being that casting director and knowing what kind of human beings, what kinds of personalities tend to fit together, and conversely, which ones don't."

Glenn makes another excellent point to build on that translates to the people you work with and work for: "It's all about bringing value. It's 'how I can serve other people?' It's 'how I can serve my clients?' How I can serve my partners. How I can serve my brokers. It's how I can serve my artists, my songwriters.

I live a life of servitude.

"And at Power Station in 1979 I learned what servitude really meant. But tied to servitude is success, in my mind. Because if you make yourself remarkably useful, and if you have the talent to back it up, or the skills to back it up, or the infrastructure to back it up, that gives you more of a shot at being successful than not having those things in place."

This is an important insight. Build a career of servitude and bringing value to everyone around you: your customers, your coworkers, and your partners.

I embrace this philosophy as both a member of a band and a leader within a company. I find it works for building camaraderie and trust, which ultimately serves me well in situations where I need buy-in or consensus on moving my ideas forward.

There is one question I've used to make sure my team thinks of first in every situation: are you being helpful?

Here's an example. A salesperson reaches out for answers about a product to help close a deal, and you've answered this question for this person fifty times over the last week.

Answer it again. And be friendly and thoughtful in your response. Help them however you can to close the deal, and speak in a language that is easily translatable to the client.

Yes, the salesperson should know their shit. That is a different point entirely. This is about how you can bring value to the company and your peers.

Another challenge is specifically knowing how to handle different personalities and get the best out of people.

Jimmy riffs on the importance of his role here: "My job as CEO of LiveOne is to get people to perform beyond what they thought they were capable of. To kind of push people, without humiliating them, but push them in a way that empowers them to succeed beyond their wildest dreams. And that can be anything from a new product feature to a vocal take. But the main thing you have to do is know the person, right? You have to know what the person's limitations are because you have to be realistic about your goals when you're pushing somebody to a vocal take or a guitar take. You've got to know what the parameters for success are, or at least have a good indication of where the borders can be. And from there you can move forward.

"But I think a lot of people go in with an ideal and not knowing the person, and it ends up capsizing the event because they start asking too much—or asking too little, which can be another thing that can get an artist or a product person bored very quickly.

"And also what you've got to have is credibility. You have to have an established, credible reputation that says to the person you're encouraging, 'Look, I know a little bit more about this than you do.' Or at least, 'I know a little bit more about the destination than you do. Let me try to help you get there.' Without offending.

"And having produced vocals for Corgan, Bill Nedley, and some of these other guys—I mean, everyone of those vocal productions is completely different. Some guys are completely confident in their skills to the point where they kind of produced themselves. Other guys are scared to death going in there, and they really gotta be cajoled and guided through the process. Every production is different. Just like every audio engineer is different.

"Some engineers appreciate autonomy. Other engineers appreciate guidance. You gotta know where the sweet spot is and how to guide that in a way that empowers them without being offensive."

Cat finds this approach works for her, too: "I'm always meeting people and taking them for who they are, finding out where they're strong, liking and appreciating them for those strengths, and trying to orchestrate it as a team in a way that allows each person to play to their strengths.

"Because we all bring something new to the table and a team is strongest when we're *allowed* to bring our strengths to the table."

Think about your role for a moment. How do you contribute and bring value to those around

you? Whether you're an executive, a team leader, or an individual contributor—the goal should be getting the best out of everyone.

Seniority should not influence your interactions and management style.

Mike shares a great story to support this: "Going back to when you graduate from school and you join the workforce in music, especially in classical music, your first gigs are with the people you graduate with. So let's consider that to be a layer of musicians. It's probably a few years thick. People graduated a year before you, a year after you. You know these people. These are the people you're entering the workforce with. These are the people that will hire you first. You'll form groups with them, that's the word of mouth. That's how you get out there.

"And above you, people have been out three years more have their own group of people. And you meet them eventually. And so now your layer cake is two levels thick.

"And there are people all the way to the most famous musicians you can imagine. Yo Yo Ma, you name it. And they're in their own layer.

"The smart musicians, and I learned this early on, don't just look up to the layers above to the work that is 'better than them.'

"I'll bring this back to business. If I were to only look up to my boss, and my boss's boss, and my boss's boss's boss, and to Bob [Greenberg]. And only look that way as a source for inspiration and advancement and success and progress, I would fail. And you see time and again that people who just look up are; they're hollow.

"So going back to music now, I met this cello player who is the most famous cello player, freelancer in New York City. He ran Chamber Music Society at Lincoln Center, he's on five or six or ten film scores every year, he made a ton of money—probably still does. But here he was hiring me to play a gig, which was great—he was pulling me up to his layer. But then kind of wanting to know what I was doing and being willing to play on the shit gigs that I was on.

"So here's a guy who had no need for me. He had been in the business twenty-five years longer than

I had, if not more, yet he's down there—I say down layer-wise—playing with these people who are just coming up. Staying vital to what was new in music, and the youthful energy that's there.

"Now you bring that into business and you know the people who are 'below you,' the people that you hire, the people that you're senior to—have at least as much energy and value as the people above you, if not more. Because they're closer to the work.

"Bob still comes to work every single day and he sits and reviews work. And he's part of it.

"And so as long as you can stay close to the work, and you can stay close to the energy that generates the work, you will always be vital. And I think the people that succeed recognize that they're always part of the work. They are player coaches. And I think that is fairly universal."

One more thing to consider about your team:

How do you decide when to keep someone on board even if they're not fulfilling all of what you expect of them?

"For me," **Jimmy shares,** "often times when I look at people that are doing less than an ideal job, I have to qualify and quantify it against, 'What would it really take to replace that person?' Or, 'Can I make the best out of this situation and move forward with what I've got?'

"But everyone's different. There are people that are great, great musicians that if you walk into the room a certain way, you've completely collapsed their bubble and they can't perform for the rest of the day. And I learned from the best: Flood and Alan Moulder, Butch Vig. Roy Thomas Baker is a great example of somebody who just is such a cheerleader for good, and what's great about a person, and doesn't get caught up in his version of music. He's there to celebrate what makes an individual unique.

"I mean, that in and of itself is a just *huge* fucking lesson when it comes to running a company. You know CEOs have big fucking egos, right? And often times they walk around like elephants and bulls with their chests puffed out. But running a company for me: it's about grace and humility and self-respect. And respect of everybody else. After two years kind of dabbling in both modalities, I firmly believe that going the route of human kindness is way more productive than, 'Here's the fucking deadline and get it done. If it's not done, you're gone.'

"Which you certainly have to say *sometimes* because you don't want to be taken advantage of. But I think if you use the first road you end up at that second road a lot less often."

Derek Richmond draws a lot from his experiences playing in bands when fostering collaboration within the cross-functional teams at Prettybird, a creative think tank for brands: "I was never an individual contributor, or a singer-songwriter composer. That wasn't my thing. I was always part of something. I was a guitar player in a band, was part of a band. I was a player but not all by myself.

"The whole thing about you have to work with others, and work well with others to make good music is the way I attribute success anywhere I've been. No matter what job it was. And using the musician's way at looking, and listening, and hearing sounds in the same way I work in teams to identify what's working and what's not working and to quickly…

"You know in bands when something's not working you don't stick with that. You just say, 'That's it' and you move on. You cut it. Because if you don't you'll never move on.

"So that certainly applies at work.

"And it applies to project management, which is really at the core of what I've always been at a job that I've worked at professionally—it's always been kind of project manager/producer.

"In order to do that well you need to identify the strengths and weaknesses of the team and the project. And those are the same things you do in bands.

"I mean, if you're playing with people that aren't good, you don't play with them that long. You're striving for people that play well. And that can contribute to making good music. Otherwise, what are you doing?

"Same thing at the job."

He continues on this theme of figuring out what works within the dynamics of band or team: "Super groups always have this stigma about them that they're not so good because they don't listen to each other; they're just doing their own thing. Whereas a band that grew and came up together, that maybe became a super group, but didn't come from all different bands and try to merge into and try to make it happen, these are bands that listen to each other and over time, as democratic as it can be—although maybe Mick Jagger *is* the leader, but maybe Keith Richards is the leader…?

"I worked on a Led Zeppelin project this year which was amazing. It was an interactive music video for the fortieth anniversary release of *Physical Graffiti*. On that project I found out that Jimmy Page is really the leader of that band, and he'll tell you that, and it came up a lot of times in the project.

"But basically, it's listening to the band and knowing what works. And if something doesn't work—just like in band—don't waste too much time trying to fix it.

Change is good.
Change is important.

"And getting that other player could be the key to your success. Finding that amazing player that can do that, rather than, 'I gotta have this guy because he's in my family or he's been with the company forever.'

"Sometimes you have to make those hard decisions and choices to make your band or your company more successful."

I'm always gonna show up early

I'm always gonna have a great attitude

No matter where I am

DO YOU REALIZE?

Having the right tools and partners

SOMETHING REALLY AMAZING HAPPENS when a rock band removes electricity from their performance equation and picks up acoustic instruments. They play the same songs, but instantly with a different feel and connection to their audience as they react to the newness of what they're hearing. It's perhaps more intimate. Maybe more raw in emotion. They're exposed and inspired.

Great artists know how to quickly adapt when their environment changes because they understand how to take advantage of the tools around them. Those tools could be the instruments they're holding or it could be the room that they're in: small club versus large theatre versus coffee shop. The tools could be the actual members of the band, or having someone completely lay out on a song to change things up.

Anurag focuses on the comparison between song creation and building solutions. He examines all of the moving parts that need unified: "I think being able to plan out a song—because I understand we're starting with the chorus, then we're going to the verse, then we're going to the bridge, then verse and chorus—having this progression at the first level, then saying I want these guitars here and the bridge over here, and want strings to come out and the horns at the end. Compartmentalize all of these different pieces, place them in different areas, basically allow me to do project management, and being able to orchestrate all of the different workflow processes in a similar fashion because I see it as this giant movement of people who are coming together in order to make something beautiful."

That's what I view business as. This orchestration of people in order to make something beautiful happen.

Derek stresses how important having the right set of tools is to his role as executive producer: "I look at writing music—mapping it out—as like creating your project schedule and your project plan. I definitely make parallels to that all the time so that you're looking at what everyone is doing and how it's contributing and how long it's going to take to get to that next point. Where are you in your rehearsal cycle for that song? What parts do we still need to nail? You certainly look at a project plan and say the same thing.

"Strictly just as a musician, I look at things that enhance my playing or the sound. So when I'm project managing or producing, I look for things, tools: scheduling tools, programs, or ways of approaching a project, and the tools to help me [get] there.

"So I'm actually gearing up as a producer, as a project manager, with tools that help me. As much as I do with pedals and what kind of gear do I need that works well.

"And I've always done that as part of a group or band. And I guess this is true for a lot of bands—if you're a metal guitar player, you can't bring that metal guitar sound into a band that isn't metal. Unless they're looking to change. Know what I mean?

"So you have to find the right instrument, the right tools, the right piece of gear either as musician or as a professional that fits with this kind of industry-style of working."

Finding partners to support and enhance your business is just as important as having all of the products and solutions on your own.

Bands often pair up to grow audiences. And the concept of friend, enemy, and frenemy is present even in the music industry.

Reid recalls: "I remember driving eight hours to open for somebody for fifty bucks in like, New Paltz. And you guys [Ominous Seapods] were probably part of this, too. We started doing gig swaps with other bands where we'd open for their crowd. You know, Percy Hill was one that we did it with. Harpoon, Disco Biscuits. You'd open for the Biscuits in Philly and they'd come open for you in Vermont.

"Although I remember with the Biscuits, being pissed off 'cause they had played their 'main gig' of the month previously and had spent their currency, and they did like a side gig for us. Whereas we had given them *our* main gig. And you know, we were bitter because we were playing some shitty-ass gig with them. [*Laughs*]"

Al also comments on the importance of networking and forging relationships with other bands: "Ever since we started playing in moe., I've always mingled with other musicians, I guess. And always networked with other musicians. I gravitate first toward the guitar player just because we have that in common, talk about guitars and sharing ideas. I want to glean as much as I can from other players.

"And whether it's about their tone, the equipment they're using, or maybe songwriting ideas, or maybe something else. But then when it comes down to actually working together in some context—cause maybe you realize you like these people, too. Get along with them. It would be fun to collaborate and do something with them. Again, I've always gravitated toward that.

"Some of it, I'm not ashamed to say, some of it, too, has to do with the growth and development part of me. Not because I'm thinking in terms of dollar signs and success so much as just personal growth and development, I guess. Because I'm always interested in learning. I figure the more interaction there is with the world around you, the more I want to know about it. That relates to the people around that are doing these things.

"And certainly when it's an opportunity to then play with the guys that were my heroes—there are baby steps to get there. You don't go from playing a house party with moe., or playing in a basement with moe. in Buffalo, to playing with members of the Grateful Dead in an arena. But over the course of time, there are baby steps to get you there.

It's just happened one step at a time, just by having an open mind and a willingness to connect with strangers and be willing to talk to people."

Take chances and play music with different people and do different things. That's why and how you end up there. Just by introducing yourself in foreign situations.

One way to get more comfortable in those "foreign situations" is simply to study your industry.

If you don't know and own the language of the industry you're in, take the time to do it.

Talk with colleagues, listen to your clients speak, go to events. But without the language as part of your toolkit, you're at a disadvantage.

Naomi talks about this and how it's helped her as a background vocalist for legendary soul singer, Sam Moore: "Let me throw this out there. When I was in high school I had some friends I went to school with that were exceptional talents that were pursuing music, theater—they had exceptional talent and they had exceptional drive. And I did not at the time think I had either to their standard. I knew I wanted to do it, I knew it was fun, I knew I wanted to work at it. I wasn't willing to give up everything to do it. And they were.

"And knowing that, when I decided to do music, and do it somewhat professionally, I decided early on there's always going to people that just have a ridiculous skill level and a ridiculous talent.

"And that's fantastic. But I'm going to have more musical references than anyone else.

I'm going to know my music, know my music history, I'm going to have a million references to draw from. I'm always going to show up early. I'm always gonna have a great attitude and no matter where I am as a chick singer, wherever you want to put me, that's going to be enough space.

"When I got the gig with Sam Moore and in the ten years or so that I got to work with one of the most legendary soul singers in history, the other women in the background vocal section that I work with are all A-list session singers, playing with some of the biggest acts in the world. You know, playing with every major band. These are people who live the dream. And that is a place where it served me because no matter who came in and out of that section, I knew everybody's part, I could get anybody through this gig. It was never a matter of ego. I was always willing to let other people have the solo—you know, give up a solo or let them shine if that was the moment in the spotlight because it was about what the gig was—it wasn't about me fighting for my time in the spotlight. And I think stepping into that gig initially, that's where all the years of training, all the years of everything I knew of how to position myself in the band, that's where it all came together.

"When I was at a Sam Moore gig and they had a background vocalist that at the last minute couldn't do the job. So Sam's manager came over to me 'cause she had met me a couple of times before and said, 'You sing, right?' And I said, 'Yes.' And she said, 'You sing the show, right?' And I said, 'Yes.' And she said, 'Could you *do* the show?' and I said, 'Sure. When?' And she said, 'In about two hours.' And I said, 'Sure.'

"Inside I was panicking. But what kept going through my brain was: my job was not to fuck it up. I'm not the star. He's the star. My job is to not fuck it up, not distract or detract from him, and to just fill it out.

"And I got on the stage and every bit of training I had my entire life from being in any show or any band—it's all about your eyes and your ears and being *part* of the band—paid off. And I nailed the gig.

"You know even from the other singers who were on the gig who'd been doing it for awhile were like, 'Wow, that was impressive. You just nailed that.' And I said it wasn't that hard.

It was just watching and listening and understanding what my job was.

"And to be able to step into that gig at that moment and to do it, was a lot easier because I had done my homework my whole life listening to music. So, whoever he was going to do on that gig, I was familiar enough with those songs. And that's what would repeatedly happen.

"Sam's very… We would do gigs and he would the day of the show say, 'Hey, I wanna do this song.' It was often the other women in the section never heard the song before. I always knew the song. It was just part of what I learned my entire life; to know that library, to be so familiar with every type of genre. He would even throw in a Broadway song. He would throw in a blues tune. He would throw in a rock tune. Whatever it was, I had the reference point, I knew the material, and I could get anybody else through it."

FAME

The different ways to
measure success

BANDS AND MUSICIANS HAVE a few go-to metrics of success: butts in seats, merch sales, overall buzz, and possibly fame and fortune. Perhaps simplistic, they're still somewhat easy to measure and learn from. The live setting for a band, though, is probably the most valuable place for testing a song—their product.

"I found that you really didn't know if you had something until you played it live," Reid confesses. "You can tell almost instantly whether a song is going to be one of your core songs or was going to be filler. But it's rare that you played a tune that felt like it was going to be filler and it wasn't, you know?

"It's like A/B testing. But with A/B testing you go for some sort of statistical significance. Given how close you are to the music, how close you are to the audience, you almost knew when a song was done whether you had something or not."

While agreeing the "outside yardstick" of measuring success is record sales and butts in seats, Jimmy says the Pumpkins looked elsewhere: "For us, once we got to know each other's capabilities, we were able to really key in on the intrinsic value of what we were doing and say like, 'We know we've been validated to a certain point, now let's put that validation in our basket. And let's see how we can *personally* move the needle forward. And how we can take the lessons of the past and the runway we've been given both culturally and economically, and push ourselves to a higher artistic ideal.'

"And I think when you get in that position— as a band or a company—I mean, that's when the Apples of the world are born. That's when a company has been validated, or a band has been validated, to the point where the culture and their audience trusts them to the point where they can go out and take chances with the knowledge that these chances have an eighty to ninety percent chance of being successful.

"Really taking big chances that *seem* like big chances from the outside, but from the inside when you're Apple, you know that those chances still have a high success rate because they're born of a wisdom that only you possess.

"That's like when we made, *Mellon Collie [and the Infinite Sadness]*, the record company was saying, 'Look, I'm gonna tell you right now.' This is Jeff [Schroeder] and Jordan [Lloyd] who are extremely fucking smart guys telling us that if we do a double CD, we're going to take all the work that we've done and burn the house down and shoot ourselves in the foot.

"And we went to them and said, 'Look, nobody understands our audience like we do. We've been out there on the road for a year and half. We've done Lollapalooza. We're telling you our audience will support a big endeavor like this.' And we were fucking right.

"But it was only because of the previous success, and the information, and the data that we were able to take into the studio, that we had the courage—or at least part of that courage was certainly born of the wisdom that we knew we'd succeed or at least it had a ninety percent chance of success. For us, it was if we do a double record the success so far outweighs the downside. Even with the record company saying it's a potential death sentence, we knew that even with the biggest downturn it was still going to be a slam dunk for us."

> *That's the type of knowledge you have to take to a business and move the needle forward. Those are the types of things that give you opportunities to make big moves.*

Sometimes early on in a career, just getting recognition is enough to signify success. It's enough to keep you moving forward. To continue building upon your passion until it eventually becomes something bigger. Glenn shares a funny story on this.

"The first record I got a physical credit for was an Ashford and Simpson record, a live album called, *In Performance*. I *think*. I think. See? It was *so* meaningful that I don't really recall it.

[*Both laugh*]

"I think that was the first one. But that was not the first record that I had ever worked on that was credit-worthy. And that was a very tough thing. Because there was never an obligation by the artist to give anybody a printed credit in the liner notes. And as an assistant engineer, gosh, I worked on albums for David Bowie, Bruce Springsteen, and The Cars. A ton of other bands. And didn't actually receive credit on the record. And it was fine. I mean, it was disappointing. I would have loved to have seen my name on there. Ever since that happened though, years later, a lot of the people that were not physically credited on the album are still recognized, product has been updated, if not on the actual cover art, certainly in *All Music Guide* and the like. But in that moment there had been a lot of albums that I had worked on in varying roles that would have been real nice to have seen my name on there. Regardless, Valerie Simpson and Nick Ashford were very kind, and made certain my name appeared on that album. And that was my *first credit*. I could not wait to go to the local record store—which, in the neighborhood I grew up in, wasn't carrying much R&B—and try to find it. Let alone try to find my name on it. But yeah, that was pretty awesome.

"That was a magic moment because it was validation. Whether it was important validation in the overall scheme of things, or one individual's enjoyment, was immaterial to a young guy who was like, Holy shit, I got my name on an album."

Naomi shares a similar sentiment to Glenn's, that getting the call because you do great work is great way to define success. But she takes that idea one step further: "I think that success for me is making music. To be able go out and sing and play music for people is a success in and of itself. *That's* the success. That's the joy of just going out and doing it. The *dream* is knowing that I've done it with people who were on my walls growing up. On the records I bought. That's not the success.

> *The success is that I'm doing it and people keep asking me to do it. The rest is just the dream.*

"Every time I do a gig that's not my project, where somebody calls me and asks me to do something, I'm so appreciative. I'm so grateful.

It's like, thank you! Thank you so much for giving me this opportunity! And if they call somebody else, I don't have an attitude. It's never my gig. It's only my gig if they *ask*.

Naomi pauses and finishes her thought with, 'Hey man, Van Halen got rid of David Lee Roth, know what I mean?'

I talked about passion and mission informing the roots of businesses and bands. The foundational components that become the culture and reference points throughout time, that someone in the company or band can point to and say, "Hey, we're not on track with what we believe in anymore."

Are you expressing success in terms of staying on your mission? Or are you more tempted by the dream? And can there ever be a way to combine both into something meaningful and fulfilling where both success and the dream are one and the same?

Naomi comes back this idea: "There's a theory, it's not mine: the truly successful and happy people are doing what they wanted to do when they were six, seven, or fourteen years old. And when I was six or seven, or fourteen, I thought I was going be either a performer or teacher. And what I do everyday in my professional career is I'm a performer and I'm a teacher. So I guess I'm successful."

So maybe living your dream is success after all.

At least for yourself as an individual, and how you can look at the personal growth of the people you work with or work for you.

Whatever the performance indicator, it's important to know what you're measuring against before you try to look back to figure out what's working or what's not. And often times a single metric doesn't tell much of a story at all. How do you know what's working?

Cat elaborates on this, bridging her experiences as a musician and marketer: "If I think about some of the shows we play, there are some shows you play because you want to expose yourself to a new audience. So we just came off of playing the NY Pop Fest. And we're definitely a bit louder than most of the other bands that were playing that festival. We were doing that for exposure, right? So for us, that was about building awareness among a group of people who may not have known us otherwise.

"When we looked out and we were playing, not everyone was digging it, not everyone was dancing. But those that were were really digging it and they were really dancing.

"So for us the measure of success was: were people exposed to us that would not have been otherwise, and of those were there enough people that were really digging it that it seemed to be worthwhile?

"In other cases we're just playing to a core. And it's a much smaller audience. But in that audience we want it to feel like there's unity of some kind, there's a community, there's a shared experience.

"If you're going to benchmark, one benchmark does not work for all. And you have to be very clear on what you're trying to accomplish and then measure against that. So is it for awareness, and are you trying to have conversion for a small sub-group of those that are aware? Or are you trying to engage a community so that there is strength in the numbers, and you do something together with the consumer you're going after? Or are there other reasons?

"I mean, I find that the larger the organization, the more myopic they get about the measurement and it's only one true measure. That is often necessary for various reasons but cannot be the only approach. You have to be able to measure based on what you're expecting and hoping to accomplish, and that that can change."

Flexibility. Adaptation. Refinement.

Even when it comes to measurement. Maybe *especially* when it comes to measurement.

Anurag talks about working with partners and his own success being measured differently based on his company's needs at the time: "I have to produce adoption, or I end up having to bring new business to the table, or I need to make revenue for the company. So there are overarching goals that are there. But as I'm being innovative or creative, I know I need to reach one of those goals. I just don't know which one it's going to be.

And as I get closer and closer, and iterative, I get feedback like, 'Oh this is great because it will help us with this product adoption goal,' or 'this will help us with revenue goal,' or 'it will help build a bridge to a partner that were having trouble with.'

"With that iterative feedback, it helps me drive toward a certain objective, but I don't know what objective I'm driving to until I'm halfway there."

This is a pretty interesting conundrum because Anurag's approach isn't necessarily "retrofitting a metric into place" as much as it's working toward defining what success means depending on the immediate needs of the business—in the moment—and seeing if your contribution addresses it. In other words, succeeding in a fast-paced environment with a shapeshifting goal is doable when there is iterative check-ins on what the top performance metric is at the time and trying to apply the "current state of progress" to those objectives in real-time.

If the response is positive, you move forward. If not, you pause, reevaluate, and adjust. Quickly.

It's like showing up to a gig and the band leader says, "Just start playing something funky like Prince with a bit of country twang thrown in like Brad Paisley. If it sounds good, the rest of the band will jump on it. If not, come up with another idea on the spot and let's see if that works. We'll just know."

Huh?

We're left with a few thoughts on defining and measuring success.

- Have a hypothesis for what you're trying to understand and test, test, and test.

- Change your metric for success if it's not the right one. It's okay. But don't change it just to make yourself "right" at the moment.

- Be comfortable with being wrong. The "right" note is only a half-step away.

HEAVY METAL DRUMMER

Specific music approaches and language in business

Jimmy laughs when I ask him if there's anything he feels particularly well-wired for in business because he's a drummer.

"That could be the beginning of a joke. Obviously I like organization, and timing for me is a big thing. I think product market timing—those things are integral for me to have a good time. I've got to have meter and tempo in methodology. Cadence is very important to me.

The same things that are important to me as a drummer are important as a business leader. Like, 'How do things *feel*?'

Often times we'll get into these conversations of, 'What does it *do*?' And okay, 'This is what is does. And here's the metrics, here's the engagement, here's how many people like it, here's how many people hit the button.'

"But I'm getting more away from that and more into a musical product definition of like: how does it feel? And, what does the *design* feel like?

"I think this product development by design as opposed to feature-based product development is right on the money. I think that's where utility gets outpaced by creativity. For me that's what makes business fun. Being able to look that there are wins happening by people who are simply making things beautiful, and making things resonant—as opposed to things are like, a better can-opener.

"That's exciting to me. That creates a place for me as an artist in the business community."

When I ask Glenn how much he applies his years of experiences to his role as a leader in a financial services company, he quickly replies: "Absolutely. Every single day, in every interaction in business—it's there. How could it not?

I have more years in the music industry than I have not in the music industry in my life. How can that not inform every decision I make, every intuition that I have, everything that's involved in it?

"I don't necessarily *like* the music business anymore. But you can't have lived in England for thirty-seven years and not picked up some of the accent. You're not going to sound like you're from Brooklyn.

"I have looked at my interaction in the music industry as absolutely key to any successes I've had in financial services. Because I bring to the game an extraordinarily unique point of view. Now whether that extraordinarily unique point of view is an asset or a liability remains to be seen."

[*Laughs*]

Naomi brings her experiences of quickly adapting when things don't go right on stage to her work. There is perhaps more value in knowing how to recover from when a plan takes a left turn, than trying to stick to the plan at all costs: "For the most part, business people, owners, corporate leadership, spend a lot of time making plans, creating metrics, and building process—that I hate—and it's because people build it and they may need to follow it. And if it doesn't fit into that process, things go bunk. And when you're a musician, you can rehearse whatever you want to do a million times. But you know what? A string could break. I could hit a dry spot in my voice and not hit the note I was gonna go for. I have a sinus infection that day and realize I have to do something a little differently. You know, the keyboard player could have lost his place in the music for a second. Anything can happen when it's live.

"And that's where the magic comes from, by the way. When you're leaning back on the chair thinking you're gonna fall and then you don't. That's what being in a band is about. I like to use that analogy for people who have never been in band. A lot of people who aren't music people are sports people. So if you're if a sports person and you ever went down to the park to play basketball with somebody, there are people who hang out every week. And the same guys play and you know the person that when you pass them the ball you know they're not going to be there. And they're gonna miss that shot every week. And then every now and then, someone you never met before shows up and you don't even have to look for them; you know he's there. And every time you pass the ball he's just there. That's the magic of being in a band.

"And while it doesn't always happen, you know what it feels like and that's why we keep doing it. So when things fall apart or derail on stage, when you're driving a hundred miles per hour on the Audubon and not sure what gear you're in, and you turn when you're coming off the exit, and you're like, "Will I make it?" That's what it's about.

"And in business, in a presentation, in building a sales plan—I'm just more aware, I think, than the other people that the magic is gonna be when it starts to fall apart. And just like any other gig, as long as you have your eyes open and your *ears* open, you just maneuver.

"If that other background vocalist is not going to sing her part, guess what? I'll sing her part. It's not about being right, it's about getting it right."

When asked how she helps her team get comfortable with this, she pauses and says: "By teaching them craft, not technique.

> *People want answers and sometimes it's not about the answer.*

"I think that when it comes to being a musician I have ample technique, ample talent, and I certainly work the craft. And when it comes to my job in sales I think I have ample talent, ample skill, and I work the craft so that my talent and my skill become that much more exceptional. And I think that's what I try to teach my team is the craft so that they have more than just a talent to rely on. Because if the technique falls apart— if you're so focused on something… You can go back to sports—not that I've ever played any in my life—but my guess is that if you're practicing that shot all day long and you've got the technique down, it still doesn't mean you're gonna get it. So the craft is: what happens when I miss the shot because I wasn't expecting an eight-foot guy to stand up in front of me?"

BEST OF YOU

Transitions and Change

THERE'S A GOOD CHANCE you weren't always doing the job you're doing right now. There's an even better chance that changing jobs or careers was unanticipated, uncomfortable, and maybe even frightening. Or maybe you ran as fast as you possibly could to a new opportunity.

You may know this already, but that's all super normal. Here are a few stories about making a jump from not only one job to another, but one profession to another. And dare I say one *passion* to another.

GLENN

Todd: What would you consider your first gig outside of music and how did you end up doing that?

Glenn: I was always self-motivated. This is something you and I have in common. It's one of the reasons why we've always been friends. We've seen the reflection of that in each other. That's always been a really cool thing.

And I've always been very entrepreneurial. I never had a sense that I wanted to work specifically in a corporate environment from the outset. From the time I was very young, I enjoyed being more of an outsider. I wanted that kind of life. I didn't want to lead the nine-to-five. Which might be a great life, but just not for me.

In being entrepreneurial, even when I was firmly situated as a record producer—and here I was making that money and working on a consistent basis, doing project after project—as you would imagine, being the networking guy that I am, and interacting with different types of people, opportunities would come up. My big goal in life after being a producer—and this was totally wrong now, but looking at from back in that day—I wanted to be a record label president because I thought everyone else did it wrong.

[*Laughs*]

Boy, was I *wrong* about that. But I wanted to do that. I kind of put it out there that that's what I wanted to do, much in the way that I put it out there when I was a receptionist that I wanted be a record producer. And that worked out pretty well, so, I was like, "Okay, what the fuck." I'm gonna start telling people I want to be a record label president.

Because I'm much smarter than these guys.

[*Both laugh*]

And then I got the gig, and boy, was I wrong about that. I did not do a great job and it was not a great space for me. But the reason I even bring this up is the one thing I learned how to do was I learned how to raise money.

And I didn't know that what I was doing was private equity. It was just, "Wow, this is kind of cool. I have an innate ability, I'm a decent salesperson, I can get my ideas across and convince people who are financially well-endowed to invest money into these ideas that I have. Holy shit, this is kinda cool."

I didn't understand fully that there is an entire branch of what happens on Wall Street that's devoted specifically to that. I was kind of foraging through the music industry. And finding people who had like-minded ideas, and again, who were financially well-endowed enough to invest in companies. That's exactly what happened.

I put together this company called American Garage. We were distributed by Navarre, which was a major distribution company. And we had great partners. The record label was not successful because record labels need to have a major star or major hit or they are not going to be successful. Also, it was formed right at that crux between records and CDs selling and not selling. And the shift to online.

This was back in 2002.

Then I also found something else out: I hated every minute that I was there.

And I didn't realize that that was what was going to happen.

Because all of a sudden I went from being a creative, who understood completely how that end of the business worked, to being somebody that could have been selling Tide laundry detergent. It didn't make a difference.

We had to buy into retail programs, we had to give extra money to Walmart for product placement. It was an eye-opening education for me. And after two and half years, I resigned, and I was miserable.

But—it taught me how to do business in a remarkably different way that was an important component of what the music industry was all about. I saw the music industry as singularly being: you go into a studio, money comes in, we create this thing and we're fucking geniuses, and of course people are going to love the work we do because it's great music. And I didn't see the behind the scenes, the kind of Oz-like what goes on behind the curtain.

And I knew about it. Of course, I knew about it. You know, there would be managers and attorneys and A&R people—but I thought they all did *nothing*. Know what I mean? And the real education, the real "walk a mile in my shoes" was great, because not only did it teach me what I didn't want to do, but it honed my skills.

It made me have a deeper understanding of what business really was all about. That we were basically—while relatively talented—assembly-line workers. Here we were putting a guitar part on a record that was like putting an engine in a car. And then everything else that happens: the dealership, the advertising, the marketing, the radio. All of those other things were not only necessary components, but remarkably *important* components.

It was a hard lesson. It was not a fun lesson. But it was still an enormous lesson.

As I moved forward, I started running around with a group of people very informally, that were angel investors. And I started spending as much time with investment-side guys—individuals, nothing corporate—people who had money. So I'm still making records and I interact with some well-known biotech entrepreneurs. They funded a production company for me that was actually quite successful. We did well. But we were also in this place where the music industry itself was losing anywhere from 10–20 percent in annual revenue overall. The handwriting was beyond on the wall. We were completely understanding that we were very lucky to be treading water and not losing money in an environment where the largest players—the Sony's, the Universal's, and the Warner's—were all losing 10–20 percent annually.

I'm out to dinner with these investors—this is about seven years ago, and we're friends now—with a gentleman who was the head of venture capital for Maxim Group in New York and a couple other people. And they had me along just as a fun dinner, a fun night out. We're sitting around talking and they don't give a rat's ass about the six-hundred-million-dollar deal that they're all talking about. They want to hear about Madonna.

[*Laughs*]

So the focus was on me and my experiences in the music industry and they really wanted to hear about it. Even my investors who have heard the same stories a million times, they were still fascinated—it was a great dinner. Long story short, the guy sitting to my right—again, the head of private equity for Maxim Group. And about halfway into our meal he's like, "You know, you would kill in private equity."

And I said, "What does that even *mean*."

"Oh you've got to pass a couple of small tests, but it's no big deal. You're a pretty bright guy. You're fairly articulate. What do you think?"

I'm like, "What do you mean, what do I think?"

This guy is offering me a job.

So I call my wife on the phone, we have a two-and-half-year-old daughter, and I say, "What would you think about this opportunity?"

And my wife—god bless her—was like, "I think you should go for it."

So, without my family, I moved to New York for a year and I became a private equity guy.

That's how I got my start. I stopped doing records entirely for that year, and I did really well. It was a really great fit.

But I do very much believe that that unique combination of the business experience I've had in my formative years in the music industry combined with a real dose of reality on Wall Street—nobody in their right mind would have done this. My life is not a game plan for anybody to follow. Nobody would take thirty-seven years in another business to then try to reinvent themselves and go into a business that, at least from appearances point of view, have no relationship to each other whatsoever—have no parallels.

But the point is: they do have all the parallels in the world. And then some.

Nothing really happens in a vacuum.

What that means for me is that when I made the transition into financial services, I really assumed that my prior life in music and everything that I had accomplished would have no relationship whatsoever to this new career path. You're learning a new language; you're learning a new narrative. There's no way these things could be more related in any way: morally, cosmically, educationally. And what I learned is that they could not be *more* related to each other. *More* dependent to each other.

It took me four years in financial services to accomplish what I did in thirty-five years the music industry. That isn't because I'm a particularly bright guy, which I'm not. It's more because I already tread that ground. I understood very quickly where I wasted time in the music business. Eliminate the word "music" and just say, "business." I made my mistakes very early on and, quite frankly, continue to do so now. But the remedy for those mistakes, the template is already there for that. Know what I mean? With the music industry, it was my first time down the road. It was my first dance. And all of a sudden I started seeing extremely familiar patterns based not only upon experience, but human interactions, very identifiable patterns that are applicable across the board.

ROB

Todd: What was the first job you got outside of pure music. Where you had a foot in something different?

Rob: I had worked with clients—the internal client and the external client—when I was doing album designs and merchandise, where other bands would come to me and ask for help. In that regard, that was a "job."

But when I was home from tour, there were a few local agencies that I would work with, basically acting as a grunt designer, doing production-based stuff. But the real "job job" that I had, and it was immediately after quitting the band, was at Cadient. Folks I had been friends with through the music scene, I just reached out to them. I said, "Hey, I know you're doing stuff in the design field. Where are you working?"

My buddy Brian Feely said, "You should come check out Cadient."

So I walk into my interview and my entire book is punk, metal, hardcore album covers, posters, and websites. And I'm thinking this is not going to work. But I was really lucky in that the guy that hired me, the creative director at the time was into music. He had played in bands his whole life. He was in punk bands. He still plays to this day. And he looks at my portfolio and was like, "I know there's nothing conservative about this. I know there's nothing in here that looks like a corporate layout whatsoever."

But he saw that I had promise and gave me a job. So I went from opposite end of the spectrum with the client thing of, "Do whatever you want. Just make sure it has a skull on it," to, "Here's this box you have to fit within. Here are your brand guidelines, here are your four colors you can work with. Here are your two fonts."

Go.

I loved the fact that I had a job because it was tough to find a job then. But after a couple months I was like, "What the hell did I do? Why did I quit this band to be doing this awful work for companies that I don't jive with." Obviously coming from a political background to big, corporate giants, I felt a little "sell-outish."

I stuck with it and I feel that I became a better designer and a better thinker after forcing myself into, "You have this box. Do what you can do within this box." And one of the great things I learned at Cadient was the strategy side of things. Every agency I had worked with prior to that—there was no sense of strategy. It was just following instructions.

At Cadient, they had an entire team of strategists that influenced the heck out of me in terms of thinking things through, looking at the category, looking at the demographic, looking at the client, and making context a big part of what you're doing. Looking at metrics and analytics to inform design.

Thinking before doing.

ANURAG

Todd: Let's get back to that moment of, "Hey, I kind of dig this, though. I kinda dig the marketing, understanding that world."

Anurag: Here's what happened. When I was young and doing the eBay stuff, that's when I kinda got into marketing. So I learned about internet ads and I was like, "Wow, if I get people to click on this they'll give me a nickel?" So I started getting into internet ads when I was younger before I found music because there was this gap of time between fourteen and fifteen where I wasn't headstrong into audio engineering.

During that time I got into DoubleClick, and after that ad networks, and affiliate marketing, and doing all that type of stuff. I didn't know what it was called, all I knew was that if I bought some advertisements for a penny and showed it in front of the right people and they clicked on it, I'd get a nickel back.

So I was doing this little-kid-game type stuff when I was younger before music. Okay, great.

But I continued my love for tech, so as I'm doing music all throughout I'm nineteen to twenty-six or so, the entire time I was reading the Facebook API. They came out with Ads API I think around 2007. So I never got access to it because it was held back, and that's what allured me more.

So I started reading about what could be done with the Facebook API just for fun, writing little computer programs here and there to pull data. It was fun, it was cool, I enjoyed it.

Then I never thought of it as a job, I was just messing around.

The moment everything changes for me is that I'm out of town—at least I tell my partners I'm out of town—and I was like, "Hey, are there any sessions in the studio?"

"Nope, no sessions."

And I walk into the studio and Girlicious—signed by Universal at the time—was recording at my studio with the songwriter that wrote Rihanna's "Umbrella," at the same time. So this is like the real, full studio session that's occurring from a major label paying for it. And it was completely swept under the table. It wasn't going to go to me. It was: they were trying to pocket it for themselves.

At that moment in time I was like, "Why am I working so hard? Why am I the guy risking all this stuff so that other people can look like the cool guy?" 'Cause I didn't care about that stuff. And they're stealing money from me. I was like, I can't handle that. I can't work at American Express and have all this overhead of all the money I ever made go into the recording unit. Because the recording fee was maybe $3,000. I must have put at least a hundred-fifty grand as a twenty-three-year-old into this. Which is ridiculous. And other people are stealing from me.

So I was like, the music industry has this low barrier to entry, not everybody is educated, people are short-sighted, they're thinking about the $10,000 now and not the million dollars later. I can't handle this anymore. I went through this: what do I want to do with my life?

So I was like, man, I wish I could work with Facebook. I really want to work there but I have no idea... At that time I had dropped out of college because I was running the studio and working at American Express. I had to let the college thing go, 'cause overtime it would be, "Here's midterms or you could go to the Grammy's. Or you could go to SXSW."

I ended up doing all those things instead of taking my test and I'd have to drop my classes before I failed. So I let go of college and I was like, I really want to work at Facebook, but how do I do it?

So what I do is at the American Express job directory, I type in, "Facebook," and one job comes out. It was for a marketing position. And it was: "Refine the way that American Express works with Facebook for card-member acquisition."

It said: "PhD required."

I was like, shit. I'm not going to be able to get this job.

But I go to the hiring manager, and I've got a good name as far being able to be technical, and I'm like, "Look man, I'm not a PhD. I'm not a statistician." They were looking for an econometrics person, which is mathematics and economics put together. And I'm like, I am not that person.

However, here's a prototype that I built of being able to work with Facebook's graph, and then being able to push it into a relational database so that you can fire SQL queries on top of it and retrieve the information in a structured format.

Nobody had done that before inside of American Express because everyone was used to SQL, which was structured query language for databases, but nobody understood the JSON Graph API that Facebook had developed. So I was the first guy to build that.

And I showed this prototype and the guy was like, "You did this?"

I was like, "Yeah, I did this by myself in like, a week."

He was like, "Okay, you're part of the team."

They dropped the need for a PhD; they gave me a promotion. I went from a Senior to a Lead. And within a week, I was on my way to London where I was being told I was hand-selected with forty other people to redefine the way that American Express and social networks were going to work together.

Suddenly I was part of this Disruptive Innovation team that was working on internet marketing.

REID

Todd: You're starting to bring in some marketing terminology. Let's talk about this transition from professional musician to marketer. What was your first gig in marketing? Were you still touring, or was it a hard stop like, "This music thing, I'm just putting it on ice for a bit?"

Reid: They say everybody has "a book." I think there's "a book" in me for sure just around this whole journey. It's been a really fascinating one and really sort of emotional one. It continues to be.

For me, Strangefolk stopped making sense primarily because it doesn't make sense to begin with, right? It's such a hard lifestyle and it's so challenging just to be on the road all the time, and I know I'm telling you what you already know. But you can make sense of that insanity if the thing that drew you to it is still whole. And that's the creative process. And the camaraderie. Basically, the dynamic of the group and how the team was functioning.

Looking back, we had what we I would call with decades of experience elsewhere, we had "structural issues" and personality conflicts from day one. But I was willing to put up with that. And for me, the creative process fell apart. It's hard to separate your own ego from the collective, but for me, I knew what I liked doing, right? I just described it. It's singing and writing songs. Because of the other member's desire to do that, I just kind of found myself boxed into a corner and I felt like if it's not fulfilling creatively, then none of this other stuff makes any sense.

If my passion is being crushed then I'm not willing to put up with the rest of the garbage. So that built for a long time, it wasn't an overnight decision. It was years in the making. And eventually I just snapped and I quit. I was done.

By the standards of the professional world, it was totally reasonable. I gave them something like four or six months, whatever it was. But it was a substantial amount of time. But it was a crushing blow to those guys. And it was nonnegotiable.

I was done.

And it wasn't me necessarily saying, like, "I quit music. I hate music." It was just that circumstance had gotten so rotten that it was unsustainable. But the notion of creating another band, having just described how laborious it was to build that band, the notion of doing it again was just unfathomable. I can't stand the one I'm in and I can't imagine creating another one, so I was completely and utterly rutter-less. I mean I had never been so lost before or since. Because everything I had aspired to be was with that band and I left it, and I had no sense of north. I had no other career desires.

I really had no framework for who I was as an individual.

So it was a really traumatic experience for me.

And my dad suggested I get a master's degree. And the aim was to (a) learn how to do something else and (b) buy some time to figure out what to do. People like hearing this in terms of a personal interest story, but those who know me as a musician found it so contradictory to who I was that I went to business school.

But I went because I felt like I had committed myself to passion my whole life, and that I owed it to myself to do something that was practical. And I felt so lost I didn't know what else to do is the honest truth.

I actually applied to just one business school. My wife was getting a nursing degree in Rochester. And I didn't want to go to business school. I didn't want to do anything. But I was like, "Fuck it. I'll apply to one school and if I get in I'll go." And this was actually while I was still in the band. This was my trigger for getting out.

We were off the road for like a month and studied for the GMAT for month straight and then took it, because you needed like two days' notice. I applied to Cornell, one school—intentionally chose a whopper—and I was like, "If I get in, I'll pull the trigger. If I don't, I won't." And miraculously, I got in.

Todd: Wow. Now you get to an incredible school. Though everyone may have seen it as the antithesis of who you were, a performer. When you got in, did you enjoy it?

Reid: No. I felt like I was hallucinating.

Todd: Did you feel like you were selling out or something?

Reid: Nope. I mean, I guess. It was so much more dramatic than that. I honestly felt like I was in a hallucination.

I went from the van to this classroom with dudes who'd come from Wall Street wearing cufflinks. I didn't know the difference between revenue and income. Literally. Did not know the difference. Just didn't know the vocabulary. I almost failed out. They took me aside and said, "You gotta decide if you want to be here or not. But you can't make F's."

I made some friends there and stuff, but I hated it. It was too much too fast, in hindsight. But I was going through my own personal grieving process, and then going through this Navy Seal business program. It fucked me up.

But I made it through. I got my act together. And the first year was much harder, and then the second year I started [the band] Assembly of Dust with a student loan from Cornell. And I made a record while I was still at school.

Todd: There was no escape, right? The gravitational pull of music still had its target on you.

Reid: Yep. So I only stopped playing for about six months. I know I'm giving you more detail than you want, but some trippy stuff happened. This one night, probably about four months into school, I decided to go play at a coffee house. Same thing, open mic. In Ithaca, unannounced. I didn't sign up, I didn't advertise. Just walked in, marked my spot. You know, there were seven people in the audience. Played my allotted three tunes. And when I got done, some dude in the audience stood up, took off his sweater, and was wearing a Strangefolk T-shirt underneath.

Anyhow, so I got this band together in school. I started playing gigs in Ithaca and around New England, made a record, and took root again.

So for me, I was just hedging for a number of years. Really the thought that occurred to me was that there were guys that I knew that were playing professionally and they did other things on the side to bring in some income. So banging nails, or masonry work, or guitar lessons, whatever. And I figured, fuck it—if they can do that I can do marketing-related shit on the side to do music.

So I set out with this dual-headed career after business school and I went to Snapple. I'll find it for you, but there's an article. *The New York Times* wrote an article how weird it was that I was working at Snapple and playing in a band—working at Snapple as a marketing brand manager and playing in a band.

I hated it. I hated the culture and the rigidity. And that's part of what I didn't like at Cornell. And then I got an opportunity to work at eMusic, which is a digital music start-up. First and foremost, it had music. That was part of it. And then it was a start-up.

Then I didn't really know what a start-up culture was. But I figured it out there. And that's when it clicked for me because the mechanics, the personalities, the ethos, the whole vibe, was so much closer to what I knew. So instead of feeling like a bifurcated person, I was able to be myself and admit that I had played in a band, used the word "fuck," and just not have to live a lie.

It was finding a business environment that afforded me that culturally, and also that fed my passion. The things that are so similar about startup life is you're defining something new, or at least attempting to, with a group of like-minded people who are singularly focused on that one thing.

That's how I found my way.

CAT

Todd: So there you are, you're teaching yourself the guitar, you're getting involved with different artists, and you've got this platform for creation. At some point you're like, "I can make a couple bucks here." There's something you can do to at least sustain that level of creativity. So even if you weren't making tons of money as a professional [musician], what made you want to go that route and not just keep making four-track recordings in your room?

Cat: I knew that [music] was probably not going to sustain me from a rent perspective. You know, I grew up in the Northeast and the cost of living is so high. It's interesting because around the time I was in college, my ex-boyfriend who was the drummer in The Best Wishes was at Wesleyan University, and he was taking a number of courses in experimental music, and Alvin Lucier was a professor there. I remember going there and watching Alvin Lucier perform some of his original pieces, and classmates of his, performing the original pieces. I was just blown away.

Part of the reason I was blown away is that behind each of those musical pieces was a big document, a thesis on what it was and what they were trying to do and how they were trying to impact you.

I loved that interplay between the artistic expression and the artistic creative intent. I just wanted to be able to that. But truth be told, I was what—seventeen, eighteen at the time—I didn't know enough about the world. I had already gone on tour a couple of times, but it wasn't as if I knew psychology or philosophy or sociology, and I really wanted to move people in that way, and to do that, I felt I had to be schooled in the humanities in order to have an educational base that would let me create something that would truly move people. So I switched to psychology so that I could understand why people do the things that do.

It was this curiosity in humanity that brought me there. I didn't want to be a psychotherapist. I didn't want to fix people. I wanted to *contribute* to an experience—not make them better. And when I had to graduate, I was asking my counselor at the time, my advisor, I said, "Listen, I need to do something. I need to get a job. What would you recommend?"

And he said, "Well, you have an artistic background and now you have psychology. Have you ever considered advertising?"

And I went into advertising at the dawn of some of the most beautiful ads out there. You know it's when Volkswagen had some of their beautiful work, and it's actually one of the reasons I met Arnold [Worldwide]—it's because of the heritage of the Volkswagen work. It was the first time I saw creative that was on television that spoke to me. And they were using things like Trio—you know there was a lot of really good music in their spots at the time.

So I went into it, and I see my job as writing that fifteen-page document that is the intent behind the creative work that creatives then do. Executing on it. That's my role as a strategist and a planner.

Todd: So your role is writing the intent?

Cat: The creative intent. Right, it's the strategic intent. So just like Alvin Lucier had that fifteen-page document that would explain his musical pieces and what he was trying to accomplish, I believe that my job today is writing those documents.

My job is to give the creatives inspiration and insight into humanity so that whatever we create moves people just like Alvin Lucier was able to move people with the pieces that he did.

DEREK

Todd: Let's start to switch gears a little bit. Let's talk about your first gig in marketing and advertising. What was it?

Derek: I started in print manufacturing and design. In college, I studied graphic design and I ended up getting involved in print design. You know, two-dimensional offset printing, sheet-fed. Either magazines, brochures, whatever. Advertising kind of material.

So we would print for advertising companies and brands. And then ultimately in the late nineties, I transitioned to work for a design studio that was the other side of that. It was the design side of what I was always printing. These were people that would do layouts for billboards, or bus wraps, or for books and magazines and magazine ads. Now I was on the other side.

But it wasn't an agency per se. It was more of a design studio. And then kind of parlayed that into—'cause we started working in the web area doing websites and banners and online media at its infancy—I started to work for an all-digital advertising agency that did websites, banner ads, and all of that for clients and brands. So I did that for about seven years. About 2001–2011 I was doing that.

Prior to that it was printing the advertising, then it was the design for the advertising, and then it was full-on the agency that came up with the ideas.

Todd: How did you end up doing that? Talk more about that progression.

Derek: I can tell you exactly how it started. I was in junior high school, I was probably twelve or thirteen. I was in print shop. We would do a lot of silk screening. We'd create silk screens, and the big thing to do, because I loved music, was to create band shirts and band posters. I'd make shirts of bands like The Police, U2, and Stray Cats—these were big bands back then.

So basically I was making merch, but I wasn't making merch to sell. It was just for myself and handing it out to friends. And that is what got me into printing.

Because not only could it be silk-screen, but it could also be lithography or actually printing booklets or magazines or whatever. That's what got me into printing.

But music and the printing of music-related stuff was what it was. It wasn't just that I was printing, right? So that goes way back.

I then went to college for printing and graphic design and layout.

When I was working at this printing company, I was there for a long, long time. And when this opportunity came to move over to the design side, it was basically like going back to the beginning of what interested me in doing print, which was the design and the layout and the graphic aspect of it. Not just executing it, but actually designing it.

I was a designer but that wasn't my role. But it was all about creating the idea. That's what got me into the design side of it. And then the web just kind of came out of nowhere.

"Oh, there's this thing called the Internet."

I can always go back to my graphic arts class in junior high and say that's what got to where I am, even right now.

Todd: It also seems like there is a mechanical component to this all, as well. There is some sort of gear involved. There is some sort of machine involved. There is a toolkit that you've progressed through.

Back to that in a second. You talk about where you ended up today. I know you were at Goodby, Silverstein & Partners for a bit and now you moved back down to LA and you're at Prettybird. How did you end up landing that gig? Talk about what you're doing today.

Derek: Just briefly, when I was at Goodby, Silverstein & Partners, I was running digital production. That led me to a job in Los Angeles, where I'm from, which was a big impetus, to be back where my family is. I got a job at another agency called 180LA running integrated production. That didn't last too long because they didn't have a lot of integrated production, they just had a lot of commercials.

So then I moved to Deutsch in LA and I was a director of digital for about a year. But being in LA, you're around a lot of things related to film and video, and I was really interested in the merging of video and interactivity, and Prettybird was looking for someone to take the company in that direction. So I moved from the agency side to the production company side.

So the place that I work was for years a traditional production company that did commercials for advertising agencies, exclusively in music videos. Music videos is a big part of what we do here. And then coming here, I wanted to do interactive video. So interactive music videos— getting back to what I really love and have a passion for.

That's what got me away from the advertising agency side and into the production company side.

LAST GOODBYE

A few parting words

I CONSIDERED STARTING THE book with this section. But I felt it was like listening to *Abbey Road* and starting with "The End" and then moving on to "Come Together." Okay, maybe not that dramatic. But really, if you started here you done good, and I admire both your brilliance and short-attention span.

I want to make sure you have a few quick nuggets of insight, clearly geared toward looking at things slightly—or totally—different than you do today. So here are my two closing questions for each interview. My Phil Donahue–Oprah–Charlie Rose questions that in retrospect, are trick questions. Or rather leading questions. I was hoping to hear similar responses to each question and in most cases I did. And it's here, in the responses from these musicians and business leaders, where you may see the most collision between these two worlds and find the most value for yourself, your work, and your passion. Open your ears and really listen.

CAT

Todd: What's your best piece of advice for business leaders, speaking as a musician?

Cat: Know who you are and what you're trying to do, but don't be afraid of changing how you end up doing that in the market.

Todd: What's your best piece of advice for musicians, speaking as a marketer?

Cat: [*Laughs*] That can go in so many different directions.

I think it's really hard to be a musician right now because the economics and the dynamics at play in music are so different than they were ten years ago. You have musicians that are extraordinarily talented and ten people come out to a show, and it can be so disheartening. 'Cause here you are, you traveled eight hours, you're on a tour, you're down to your last ten dollars, and you get thirty dollars at a show that you have to start asking yourself, is it worth it?

I think my best advice is that...success can be defined differently and sometimes having that one person who's at a show and you've touched their life in a way that makes it all worthwhile, that the measure of success for a show should not be measured in the money you get or the size of the audience that comes out.

ROB

Todd: What's your best piece of advice for business leaders, speaking as a musician?

Rob: Collaborate. To not put everything on your shoulders and do it alone. Build a community of folks that you trust and cherish and that you would go into battle with. By building that community and building that group of people you have trust in, and that are all passionate, you're going to exponentially grow your potential.

Todd: What's your best piece of advice for musicians, speaking as a business leader?

Rob: I have a buddy that runs a record label. He put out one of BoySetsFire's first records. He runs Magic Bullet Records. He's an outstanding human. I always see these things on Facebook where he's talking about new, upcoming bands. And they don't even call them demos anymore, they call them "applications." "I'd like to send you an application, "like they're applying for a job. It's become this whole clinical, "A+B=C." I think that the punk rock and hardcore community still exists and thrives—maybe not below the radar like it used to considering everything is connected nowadays.

He said it best, "Just be prolific. Just make. Just *do*." If it's good—or even if it's not good—the fact that you're making and being creative, it has a net-positive outcome. But as far as people who want to gain traction and be popular, it's not about getting the record deal. I keep going back to community, but it's what made BoySetsFire and every other band I've been involved with successful. If you're putting out music, you're being prolific, and you're playing; the other half of that has to be the community aspect of it. Which is: connect with bands from two cities up the turnpike or two states away, and start booking shows for them. Get them to come your shows. To your venues. The more you can help other bands out and building that community, the outcome from that is that people will start hearing about you. They'll start gaining interest because there will be a real current of positivity about you.

ANURAG

Todd: What's your best piece of advice for business leaders, speaking as a musician?

Anurag: Strive to make something beautiful. Don't just strive to put dollars on the line and move the needle from 60 percent to 62 percent. There's a time for putting your head down and working on something, and there's a time for going, "Here's what we're doing today in the best way that we can do it."

You know, take 20 percent of your time and think, "If I was to smash everything to the ground and build something new, could I build something more beautiful than pieces that I have?"

Todd: What's your best piece of advice for musicians, speaking as a marketer and technologists?

Anurag: You can make music for the rest of your life and be completely happy with that, and that's fine.

But if you want to jump into the music business, learn business. Understand you have to be somewhere six months from now, two years from now, twenty years from now. If you're playing the same gigs in the same bars and talking to the same people, you're not doing things the right way.

If your vision is to play Madison Square Garden, then you really need to back up how you're going to get there and take a business approach to every day, of becoming better, building more connections, and working toward that process.

And if you're not getting there? Pivot. Switch. And switch quickly and iterate. But if you stagnate, and if you don't focus on business, then you might be good at music but you'll never make it in the music business.

GLENN

Todd: What's your best piece of advice for business leaders, speaking as a musician and producer?

Glenn: It's the thing I personally struggle with the most, which is listening. I know it sounds very simple, but it is listening. I think as human beings, as a matter of survival we have to run things through our own filters. And we tend to hear things based upon what our past experiences have been. I think the thing I struggle with the most is getting out of the way of myself, and really *hearing* what other people are saying.

When I say it's a struggle, it's not a struggle to my detriment. It's more of a struggle in that I have to make myself consciously aware that when I disagree with somebody, or my knee-jerk reaction is negative to something that has been put in front of me, it's almost like I have to push that button and say, "Wait a second. Give this a chance. Give this some opportunity. *Hear* what this person is saying."

Todd: What's your best piece of advice for musicians, speaking as a business leader?

Glenn: I'd say to people who want to be in entertainment in general, whether it's as a performer or support role, that it's always been a very, very tough place to make a living. Always. Historically, if the court jester didn't please, they'd cut of their head. That's a pretty tough audience. I'd suggest in modern times it's only gotten more difficult. People tend to think that the ability to generate interest in terms of social media has democratized the music industry and entertainment industry. I think it has devalued the entertainment industry because it's put everybody in the audience now on the stage.

All the gatekeepers and tastemakers are gone.

It's communism. I'm not saying that as a political devote or anything. It's the lowest common denominator being elevated to equal level with things that actually do have value. My point is to have realistic expectations as to what can and cannot be accomplished—it's a far more difficult place to tread water than it was when I got my start. I feel bad for people starting out right now because the challenges are greater. If we won back in the day, then there would be significant financial remuneration, there would be a very definable arc for career, definable marketing, very definable touring opportunities. A lot of that has been diluted or may not exist anymore—you may starve. But far be it for me to tell anybody not to follow their dreams because I have done exactly the opposite of what I'm advising right now. I did follow my dreams. And because I followed my dreams I got to meet you. I got to make a record with you. And I got to reconnect with you some ten years later and now work on this book with you. So I think I'm a living example of hypocrisy.

[*Both laugh*]

I'm telling you that you shouldn't be doing this, yet I'm living this privileged life in that we do get to interact on so many different levels, then I'd be the first one to say that my advice is foolish and should not be listened to at all costs.

[*Both laugh*]

REID

Todd: What's your piece of advice for business leaders, speaking as a musician?

Reid: Pick what genre of music you're playing. I think business leaders are afraid to commit to an audience because they're afraid of making the wrong choice. And authentic musicians do it because it's who they are. And I found those who were able to commit decisively—GoPro as an example; Phish and the Grateful Dead as an example—succeed because at least they deliver something to someone.

And where I think a lot bands and a lot businesses fail is trying to be everything to everyone.

Todd: What's your piece of advice for musicians, speaking as a marketer?

Reid: Well, I've got a shit-ton of advice for musicians.

[*Laughs*]

One is that I believe you make your own luck by working hard and being smart and being good. So that's one. I don't believe the old adage that lucky people succeed in the music industry.

Two is be as good as you can possibly be. And that refers to both your art and the commerce that surrounds your art, if you're serious about making a living out of it. Because where I think most musicians have failed is—and it's where I think the old music industry is flawed—is saying, I'm an artist and I'm going to put my well-being—my career, basically—in somebody else's hands because they're either interested in that, or they're better at that than me, or they're smarter than I am, or just whatever. I don't want to be bothered by it.

And that old cliché, idiot-savant-artist-thing just doesn't float. There's no excuse for not being good at the business of music. Again, with few exceptions—sure there are the Ozzy Osbornes of the world. And that is lucky. He's lucky that he found a wife who's supportive and smart in the business world. But maybe he's not lucky. Maybe he was smart. And maybe Warren Haynes [The Allman Brothers Band, Gov't Mule] was smart by finding a partner to support him.

Mick Jagger is famous for being great at understanding and being involved with the business. U2 is run like a major corporation.

That's my advice.

Don't discount operationalizing and marketing your business.

Because that's what it is. Unless you're doing it for fun. And then don't be naive and think you're going to be successful financially.

AL

Todd: Having your musician hat on, what's your best piece of advice for business leaders?

Al: My first inclination is to say to listen. Not only to their "fan base" in whatever context that may be, their peers, their coworkers. Because listening becomes so integral to what we do in terms what you want to put forth. Because if you're just talking all of the time, or in my case, just playing all of the time, then I'm not in a band anymore. I'm not working together anymore and utilizing the strengths and skills of the musicians of my band.

Todd: What's your best piece of advice for musicians speaking as a business leader?

Al: I don't know how to say this without sounding trite: there should be integrity in their work. It's so easy to lose sight of that, especially in the world that we work in. But it's really important that at the end of the day we're doing work— and I'm not talking about the music as much as I am the business decisions that we make—there needs to be integrity in those decisions. In that you're establishing long-term relationships with people and treating people fairly and kindly.

And whether that be your customers, your peers, your associates, or your clients—it doesn't make a difference.

But if you do that work with integrity there is much more chance of succeeding and lasting, I would think than otherwise.

Without it sounding too much like a Boy Scout motto, it's difficult to do a lot of times but it's something we've learned along the way. We strive to maintain those relationships with people, and work together with people, and not burn bridges. All of those things. It's very important to us. And it's probably why we're on the very slow trajectory that we're on. We've never seen a huge rise or growth in what we do. But we've also never knowingly fucked anybody over. And we won't. We refuse to do it.

There's something to be said for the people who are able to do that and are very successful at that. Because business is business at the end of the day. And for us, there's more to it than that because we're doing something that's more important— well, I don't want to say more important than business. But the integrity of what we do becomes important to us, I guess.

That's the paradox. Because you're trying to run a successful business, and if it's at the expense of the business or the bottom line, then what are you doing? And I know that probably flies in the face of a lot business rules, but for us it's been integral to our success and longevity.

NAOMI

Todd: What's your best piece of advice of advice business leaders, speaking as a musician?

Naomi: Learn how to listen. Because you never know what mistakes you're gonna hear that are actually magic.

Todd: What's your piece of advice for musicians, speaking as a business leader?

Naomi: Don't forget you're a business person. I have so many musician friends that just want to be artists. But there's still a business. If you're a musician, you're dealing with business people. Whether you're trying to book a local club, or dealing with a label, dealing with a PR company—whatever it is. You're dealing with business people and those people will be used to dealing with musicians. But if it takes you twenty-six emails to give them what they need, you're gonna drop down on their priority list.

The business piece is learning how to work with people to give them what they need to help you in the most efficient way.

JIMMY

Todd: What's your best piece of advice for business leaders, speaking as a musician?

Jimmy: This is something I know: When you're backstage at the United Center and it's sold out, you might think that everybody is back there high-fiving each other. But what they're really talking about is when the van broke down in Montana, and everybody only had twenty dollars to get it fixed.

So my advice for business leaders is:

> ### *Don't get consumed with the destination because the journey is the fun part.*

When you're sitting on a boat in the Mediterranean, you're not sitting there talking about sitting on a boat. You're sitting there talking about how you got the fucking boat.

[*Both laugh*]

Appreciate the journey cause that's where the fun is. 'Cause it gets complicated! As the Pumpkins got to be more successful, it got complicated and you sort of yearned for those simpler days when the only thing you had to worry about was writing a great song.

That stuff gets murky later on when you've got managers, and astrologers, and jets, and everything else around the company. The music becomes secondary, or subservient to economics and other things. The early times in a company's lifecycle are where the celebrations are going to be remembered.

Todd: I'm sure you can anticipate my follow-up. What's your best piece of advice for musicians, speaking as a business leader?

Jimmy: Fuck, keep practicing, man. [*Laughs*]

I mean, really listen to as much music as you possibly can. Because you never know when you're gonna pull out that crazy Weather Report part and make a song like "Tonight, Tonight," a great piece of music.

THANK YOU, GOODNIGHT!

Final Thoughts

ONE THING BANDS AND artists love about being on the road is that after the final note is played at a performance, and the crowd goes home, and the gear is packed up, they get to put on a show all over again the next night somewhere else and then again the night after that. And they need to bring the same freshness to the music and performance as they did the night before. The expectations of their fans didn't diminish overnight, right? In fact, the expectations grew because fans probably heard how incredible their show was the night before on Facebook. The stakes exponentially increase to perform better and better each night throughout a tour, and to connect so deeply with the audience that people leave inspired and emotionally fulfilled. Not to mention as a band, each member wants to feel energized and feed the desire to work as a united force of nature to make an impact on each fan. Every. Single. Show.

Imagine trying to sustain that energy and approach for fifty shows in a row. One hundred and fifty shows.

Two hundred and fifty shows or more in a year. For some bands and artists, it's even more than that when they go on a world tour.

This is not an easy thing to do. It burns people out. It causes bands to break up. In some cases, people have died on the road.

I'm not saying that if you don't have the capacity or tenacity for sustainability in your business that your head of finance is going to keel over from an Excel overdose, or your lead developer is going to get into a fist fight with your product manager because they disagree on the scope of a project that never seems to end (though I've seen people get really close on that one). But the themes of growing expectations both internally and externally are real, always present, and simply never go away.

How you choose to create an environment for your company to weather both the good and not so good may be the difference between having a one hit wonder and then breaking up the band, or being a consistent hit maker that continues to draw from the original passion to create something new and meaningful over and over. Every. Single. Quarter/Half/Year.

Are you going to continue when the cofounding drummer quits the band? What if no one is streaming your new music or downloading your album? Or rather, what if the founder and CEO decides to move on? Can you go on without her? What if a product the entire team believes in just flops? What then?

Is your company set up for resilience? And what helps make a company resilient anyway?

Here's one thought (or motif?) on what helps: when everyone at your company believes that what they're doing has meaning. That the meaning is clearly articulated, understood, and shared. That the people there connect to that meaning through both their work and life, and is central to everything they do. To be clear, not that work is central to everything they do. But that the meaning that fuels your company's mission is.

Hey, wait a sec. I believe we just finished side two of the record and it's time to flip it back over and start this thing all over again.

ACKNOWLEDGMENTS

WORKING ON A SINGLE project for more than a few months is foreign to me. I've always thrived in environments where you quickly prototype something, test it, learn from it, and then either kill it or go bigger—whether that was in music, marketing, or tech. So for me, working on this book for almost two years was an exercise in patience and trust in an unfamiliar process. But going through that new process exposed me to an industry I was not well-versed in. That's a really great thing. What got me through in one piece was being able to rely on a team that knew what it was doing to pull this all together. It's what they do. And thank god, because I certainly had no clue about all the moving parts and how to put them all together.

And here we are.

Tyson and Team Rare Bird. What an amazing partnership. Thank you for making this real.

Without getting into "Grammy speech" territory and the pit band playing me off-stage, I have a few more thank yous beginning with the generous, talented, and amazing folks I interviewed: Rob, Jimmy, Reid, Anurag, Cat, Mike, Naomi, Glenn, Derek, and Al.

Thank you. This book would not exist or sing without your voices.

There are a handful of folks who have either mentored me, inspired me, or just helped make me a better person simply by knowing them. Some of these kind souls are: Sandy Dondici, John Percival, Cat Spurway, Tom Pirozzi, Greg Nash, Bryan Lasky, Benjie White, Scott Bernstein, David Simon, Dean Pascarella.

Thanks to my parents who somehow managed to be okay with their son dropping out of a Master's program to join a rock band full-time. Thanks to my mom for teaching me how to connect with people, and be warm and open. Thanks to my dad for playing me Led Zeppelin for the first time, bringing me to work when I was a kid to "see how ads are made," and for being my first exposure to the music and business worlds beautifully colliding.

Thanks to my sister for being so supportive and encouraging through each iteration of my life. You are amazing.

Thanks and love to my two boys for being thoughtful, kind, loving, and inspiring me to do more and strive to be a better person every day.

And the biggest thanks and deepest love go to my wife, Angela.

Ange—we've toured as bandmates. You've known me as a young, struggling musician. You watched me teach myself how to code and lovingly made fun of me as I made a ball bounce with a few lines of code. You encouraged me when I was unsure if I could make a living in digital marketing, and supported me through a tough transition out of music. We've been through so much together and this book would not be possible without that support and love.

And finally—thank you for picking up the book. I hope you find these lessons from the road as valuable as I imagine them to be.

[*Cue the pit band*]

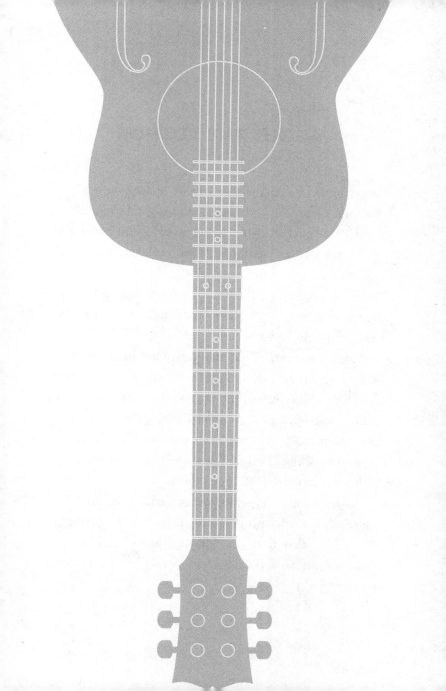

ABOUT THE AUTHOR

AFTER BEING A PROFESSIONAL musician for over ten years (writing, recording, producing, touring internationally) Todd Pasternack had the unbelievably good fortune of becoming just as passionate about creating with code and technology as he was with musical instruments. Todd transitioned full-time into digital marketing design, development, and ultimately strategy and product development.

Over the years, Todd has consulted on advertising technology for brands and agencies such as Ford, Apple, Showtime, Nike, American Express, Coke, R/GA, W+K, BBDO, and built and grew relationships with strategic, technology, and publisher partners such as Facebook, Microsoft, Adobe, Twitter, Comcast, *The New York Times, Wall Street Journal*, CBSi, and others.

When Todd isn't geeking out on ad tech, he's spending time with his wife and two sons in Palo Alto, California. You might also find him playing guitar and singing alongside his wife on bass and vocals in one of their music projects.